WHAT ARE WE WAITING FOR?

WHAT ARE WE WAITING FOR?

A Commentary on Revelation

Robert H. Mounce

WILLIAM B. EERDMANS PUBLISHING COMPANY
GRAND RAPIDS, MICHIGAN

Copyright © 1992 by Wm. B. Eerdmans Publishing Co.
255 Jefferson Ave. S.E., Grand Rapids, Mich. 49503

Printed in the United States of America

Library of Congress Cataloging-in-Publication Data

Mounce, Robert H.
What are we waiting for? : a commentary on Revelation /
Robert H. Mounce
p.   cm.
Includes index.
ISBN 0-8028-0613-9 (pbk.)
1. Bible. N.T. Revelation — Commentaries. I. Title.
BS2825.3.M7   1992
228′.07 — dc20   91-45243
CIP

Scripture taken from the HOLY BIBLE: NEW INTERNATIONAL VERSION.
Copyright © 1973, 1978, 1984 by the International Bible Society. Used by
permission of Zondervan Bible Publishers.

Contents

Contents

Introduction

When John wrote the book of Revelation and sent it to the seven churches of Asia, he fully intended that they would not only read it but that they would understand it as well. Granted, it is written in a literary style that seems a bit strange to the twentieth-century reader. But that is because most of what we read in today's press is somewhat prosaic. As contemporary Westerners we are more at home with straightforward narrative than with dream sequences and elevated rhetoric.

Not so in Judaic culture around the time of Christ. The oppressive and blasphemous rule of the Syrian despot Antiochus Epiphanes (mid-second century B.C.) led to a surge of Jewish literature in a style of writing that we now call apocalyptic. It spoke of the coming intervention of God into the affairs of man* to bring to a close the present age. It was written in a highly symbolic style.

While Daniel in the Old Testament and Revelation in the New are the best canonical examples of this literary genre, the greater part of apocalyptic writing is found outside the Bible (for example, 1 and 2 Enoch, Jubilees, and the Apocalypse of

---

* I use the word *man* here and in what follows as meaning "human being," whether male or female. When the word *man* is used in this generic sense, pronouns referring to *man* must also be understood as having this generic sense.

Abraham). It is a literature characterized by dreams and visions, often mediated by angels and normally dealing with the end of the world. It professes to reveal what is taking place in the supernatural realm.

Apocalyptic literature uses words in a distinctly symbolic fashion. In Revelation, for example, we learn that stars are angels and lampstands are churches (1:20), that the seven heads of the scarlet beast are not only seven hills but also seven kings (17:9), and that the waters on which the great prostitute sits are peoples, multitudes, nations, and languages (17:15). These interpretative clues from the book itself help to determine our approach to the understanding of such unusual sights as a fiery mountain thrown into the sea (8:8), a cloud of locusts with human faces and tails that sting like scorpions (9:7-10), and a seven-headed, ten-horned beast that arises from the sea (13:1). To interpret such visions as if we were reading the morning newspaper is bound to lead us to a distorted understanding of what the book of Revelation is all about.

Who, then, can understand this crucial book which professes to tell us of the consummation of the age? Scholars differ from one another almost as much as do their more popular counterparts who tour the country with multicolored charts and definitive answers for every detail of the book. Obviously everyone cannot be right. Must we choose between the available experts and let it go at that?

The answer is No. It is my contention that anyone can grasp the basic message of Revelation if the book is approached in the right way. Usually we get along fine in the first chapters, which take us through the seven letters and the great throne room scene. It is when we find ourselves in the subsequent chapters with their cosmic disturbances and grotesque creatures that we lose our balance. We stumble on the details. We wonder what each specific item intends to say. In time we give up in desperation.

How should the book be approached? May I suggest a

simple idea that can be of significant help in establishing a more satisfactory approach? Take a modern speech version of Revelation, get settled comfortably in your favorite chair, and read the book thoughtfully from beginning to end. Unless you pause to decipher some enigma you will find that it will take about an hour to read the entire book of Revelation.

Now put the Bible aside, take pen and paper, and jot down what impressed you as the major themes of the book. I will be surprised if you do not come up with at least the following: the sovereignty of God over forces both natural and supernatural, the fierce antagonism of Satan and his henchmen toward the people of God, the return of Christ and his victory over the forces of evil, the judgment that will fall upon those who have followed the beast, and the everlasting blessedness of those who belong to the Lamb.

But is there not more to the book than that? Yes, but everything relates to these fundamental themes. Revelation is a call for endurance for a people about to enter a period of severe persecution. It counsels them to remain faithful to the end. It provides encouragement by keeping before the people of God the indisputable fact that as history draws to a close they will share in the victory of the Lamb. The persecution in John's day came from the Roman empire; the persecution of the last days will arise from totalitarian secular authority arrogating to itself the allegiance of all people.

Revelation is not a chronological timetable for the last days. It should not be read as if its purpose were to disclose the exact sequence of the final events in human history. Revelation is more like an abstract painting than a blueprint. To interpret figures of speech as if they were literal descriptions is to misunderstand the intent of the author. It is neither good sense nor honoring to God to read the poetry of Scripture as if it were narrative.

Every style of literature has its own specific hermeneutic. We recognize this in normal conversation but tend to forget it when we come to Revelation. When we read in Revelation 21:16 that the Holy City is a cube measuring "12,000 stadia" (about 1,400 miles in all three directions), there is a tendency on the part of some to feel that to envision a city of any lesser size would amount to unbelief in God's ability to do whatever he wants to do. But the crucial consideration is whether John is asking us to believe in a literal city with those precise dimensions. Is it not possible that the dimensions are intended to recall the cube shape of the inner shrine of the temple? The New Jerusalem is cube shaped because like the Most Holy Place it is where God meets with man in love and forgiveness. Any geographical location is beside the point.

To interpret Revelation properly requires a sympathetic imagination. Its beauty is revealed to the humble in heart who wish to see the larger picture and learn the eternal truths enshrined in a style of literature now quite foreign to our ears. Details are helpful primarily as necessary parts of the larger picture. When they become the center of our interest the larger picture is distorted.

Unfortunately, commentaries tend to spend more time on the particulars than on the overarching themes. Linguistic spadework is vitally necessary for a critical understanding of the text. But it is only the first step. It is my prayer that in this commentary I have provided a balance between what the text is saying and what the author wishes to impress upon our hearts and minds. Textual observations are the basis for informative insights. Every commentator worth his salt does all he can to clarify exactly what the text is saying. But this is only preparatory to the central task of biblical interpretation — specifically, what does it mean? If this commentary leads you to reflection on the truths behind the particulars it will have accomplished its aim.

ROBERT H. MOUNCE

Revelation 1

1-3   Many people assume that the book of Revelation deals almost exclusively with the return of Christ. They are surprised to find that the Parousia (the Second Coming) does not enter the account until chapter 19. And even there it is dealt with in a few short verses that describe the event in a somewhat different way than does the more familiar passage in 1 Thessalonians (4:14-17).

The book of Revelation is not so much an unveiling (that is what the word "revelation" means) of Jesus Christ as it is a revelation made possible by him. In chapter 5 we will learn that only the Lamb is worthy to break the seals on the scroll of destiny and disclose how it will all turn out. No one else can serve as the agent of revelation.

Note that John, who is a vital link in the chain of revelation, testifies to **everything he saw.** The many visions from chapter 4 on to the end of the book were actually seen by John. They are not his attempts to put some of his ideas into a contemporary literary genre that we now call apocalyptic.

Like his master Jesus Christ, John is a faithful witness (cf. v. 5). No wonder those who would **read** the prophecy and **take to heart what is written** could be called **blessed.** Persecution was just around the corner. In fact, Antipas of Pergamum had already died as a martyr (2:13). It is a source of eternal blessedness to know that in spite of all earthly and Satanic opposition,

God remains sovereign. At the appointed time he will put an end to evil and reward those who have been faithful to the end.

4-5a In ancient days letters began with the name of the writer. This letter is from **John** (the apostle, I believe) and is sent to **seven** specific **churches** in the Roman province of Asia, the western part of modern Turkey. In chapters 2 and 3, we will find a series of seven brief letters, each addressed to a separate church. But all seven will accompany the main body of the book as it is circulated to each church. In fact, the seven letters become an essential part of the entire book. The seven cities form a rough geographic circle and were perhaps major postal centers in Asia. As such they could serve as distribution points for the surrounding areas. Revelation was for the entire church scattered throughout Asia.

The **grace and peace** pronounced upon the churches stems from a threefold source. God the Father is portrayed as existing in all time (past, present, and future), and Jesus Christ is shown as the faithful witness, resurrected from the dead, and sovereign over the kings of the earth (vv. 4-5). Each title is intended to support and encourage the believer in the coming trial, when secular power will demand that everyone worship the emperor. Some writers think that the **seven spirits before his throne** represent the Holy Spirit (Isa. 11:2 is usually quoted), but it is better to take them as heavenly beings (see the three other places where they are mentioned — 3:1; 4:5; 5:6).

5b-8 It is characteristic of the prologue and the epilogue (1:1-9 and 22:6-21) to place a series of separate yet related statements side by side. In verses 5b-8 we find a doxology, an exclamation regarding Christ's second coming, and a declaration by God of his eternal existence.

The doxologies of Revelation (and there are many them: 4:11; 5:9; 12-13; 7:10; etc.) are spontaneous outbursts of praise and gratitude. The first doxology is directed toward Christ, **who**

loves us (present tense) **and has freed us from our sins** (accomplished in the past). Christ has set us free by his death. The children of Israel were set free from bondage in Egypt and promised on Mount Sinai that if they would keep the commandments of God, they would be "a kingdom of priests and a holy nation" (Exod. 19:5-6). In a "second exodus," Christ frees believers to be the new people of God.

The return of Christ will be seen by all (v. 7). No secret rapture here! As Jesus said, "All the nations of the earth . . . will see the Son of Man coming on the clouds of the sky" (Matt. 24:30). The **peoples of the earth** (unbelievers) **will mourn,** not out of repentance, but because his return will set into motion the judgment of God (16:9, 11, 21).

Alpha and **Omega** are the first and last letters of the Greek alphabet. From the beginning of time until the end, God is in complete control of all that happens. In times of great crisis it is crucial to remember that he is **the Almighty**.

9-11   John had been exiled to the **island of Patmos,** a small, rugged island in the Aegean Sea, about fifty miles southwest of Ephesus. Apparently his preaching was making it difficult for the local authorities to propagate emperor worship, so they banished him. On the Lord's Day he received a divine commission to write down what he was about to see and to send it to the seven churches of Asia.

John identifies himself closely with his Christian brothers and sisters on the mainland. He shares with them the **suffering** involved in fidelity to Christ and the hope of a future **kingdom** of blessedness.

The **Lord's Day** was the first day of the week. It is his day because on it he rose victorious over death. To be **in the Spirit** means to be caught up in meditation about the things of the Spirit. While in this state of spiritual exaltation, John hears a **loud voice,** clear as a trumpet, instructing him to write what he sees and to send it to the churches on the mainland. The seven

3

churches are not only historic congregations. They also stand as symbols of the strengths and weaknesses of churches throughout time. They do not predict seven successive periods of ensuing church history.

12-16 What a surprise when John turns to see the one who has spoken to him! There in the midst of seven golden lampstands stands one **like a son of man,** priestly in dress and overpowering in appearance. He holds **seven stars** in his right hand and a **double-edged sword** in his mouth.

Many writers go into great detail to show what each descriptive phrase symbolizes. It is more important for our purposes, however, to reflect on the total impact of the vision than to research the possible background of each item. The total vision is of one dressed in a long robe with a golden sash, having burnished feet, pure white hair, penetrating eyes, and a deep vibrant voice. What an impact this awe-inspiring figure must have had on the venerable old disciple!

17-20 John's reaction to the encounter was to fall to the ground. He is immediately reassured by the sovereign Lord and commissioned to record the visions he is about to receive. During the earthly life of Jesus, the apostle John had a similar experience. On a mountaintop he watched the transfiguration of Jesus. A voice from heaven spoke, and "when the disciples heard this, they fell face down to the ground, terrified." Jesus touched them and told them not to fear (Matt. 17:1-8).

In verse 8 God referred to himself as "the Alpha and the Omega." Jesus makes the same claim with the parallel expression, the **First and the Last.** Both titles emphasize sovereignty. Everything is under divine control. Having conquered death through the resurrection, Jesus is now **alive for ever and ever.** As the keeper of the **keys of death and Hades,** he has complete control over their power to terrorize and enslave.

Verse 19 is often taken as setting forth a threefold outline

4

for the book of Revelation. **What you have seen** is said to refer to the vision just experienced. **What is now** would refer to the seven letters of chapters 2 and 3. **What will take place later** is understood as referring to everything from chapter 4 on. Unfortunately, the book does not fall into such a neat pattern. It is better to take the first clause as a repetition of the earlier command ("Write on a scroll what you see," v. 11) and the other two clauses as explanatory — that is, spelling out what it is that John is to see and to write (the past tense, "what you have seen," anticipates the visions that follow).

Our first clue to the interpretation of the book comes from Christ himself. The **seven lampstands** are said to be the seven congregations to which the book is being sent. The **seven stars** are seven angels (or messengers) of the churches, a reference to the local elder of each church or possibly to the prevailing spirit of each congregation.

Revelation 2

Chapters 2 and 3 consist of seven letters addressed to seven different churches in the Roman province of Asia. Since all seven are sent to each congregation, they may be considered as letters within a larger letter. When they are placed side by side a striking similarity of form emerges. With only a few minor exceptions, each letter contains (1) a command to write, (2) an identification of the author, (3) the acknowledgment of positive achievements, (4) words of encouragement, censure, counsel, or warning, (5) an exhortation to hear, and (6) a promise to the overcomer. While the letters are tailored to the immediate needs of the seven historical churches, they reveal at the same time the strengths and weaknesses of the church universal.

1 Note that in each letter the author (the glorified and triumphant Christ) is identified by a particular phrase or clause taken from the opening vision of chapter 1. For example, to Ephesus he is presented as the one who **walks among the seven golden lampstands** and **holds the seven stars in his right hand.** Taking a clue from Revelation 1:20, we understand this to mean that Christ is present in the midst of the congregation and holds them in his control.

2-3 Ephesus was a hard-working church that had maintained doctrinal purity. In a day when churches were frequently infil-

6

trated by self-styled apostles intent on manipulating local congregations for personal advantage, Ephesus had put them to the test and rejected all pretenders. Commitment to Christ had resulted in economic and social hardships for the membership, yet they had persevered and had **not grown weary.**

4-6 It has been said that a person's greatest weakness inevitably lies in the area of his major strength. This was true of the congregation at Ephesus. The ability of the church to detect doctrinal deviation had created a climate of suspicion. Love was noticeably absent among its members. The major fault of the believers at Ephesus was that they had **forsaken** their **first love.** That initial surge of love for God and therefore for one another had declined. Thus Christ admonishes them to **remember** the warm devotion of former days, **repent** of their coldness, and do those things which flow naturally from a context of love and concern. If not, he will come in judgment.

Then, lest the censure seem too severe, he commends them for hating the **practices of the Nicolaitans** (a heretical group that wanted the church to work out a compromise with paganism).

Their suggestion was that believers go ahead and take part in pagan religious festivals, eating food that had been sacrificed to idols and indulging in sexual immorality (for evidence of the same sect in Pergamum and Thyatira see 2:14-15, 20).

7 Each letter contains the exhortation, **He who has an ear, let him hear what the Spirit says to the churches.** It is crucial that believers actually hear (that is, hear and take to heart) what the Spirit says. Note that while Christ dictates the letter, it is the Spirit who speaks to the inner being. To **overcome** is to obey what the Spirit says. And to the overcomer, Christ gives the right to eat of the **tree of life** (a symbol of immortality; see Gen. 3:22-24). This is a promise to restore the fellowship with God enjoyed by Adam and Eve before the Fall.

8-11 The letter to Smyrna is the shortest of the seven. Unlike the others (except the letter to Philadelphia) it contains no note of censure. This is significant in view of the fact that the city of Smyrna was exceptionally pro-Roman and that Christians living there had already experienced intense opposition. The most famous early church father to be martyred was the elderly Polycarp, the "twelfth martyr in Smyrna."

Christ identifies himself to the believers in Smyrna as **the First and the Last, who died and came to life again.** This assurance of divine sovereignty and victory over death would be a source of strength for the church as it faced the difficult period lying ahead. Christ is fully aware of their **afflictions** and **poverty.** Apparently their faithfulness to the gospel had already brought economic hardship. Yet spiritually they were rich.

Christ also knew the slanderous accusations of those who claimed to be Jews. We recall Paul's teaching that a real Jew is not simply the one who has undergone the outward act of circumcision but the one who has experienced the inward cleansing of the Spirit (Rom. 2:28-29). These slanderers belong to the **synagogue of Satan,** not the synagogue of God. A powerful denunciation of the local Jewish settlement!

The believers at Smyrna were about to enter a new and increasingly difficult period of suffering. They were to be cast into prison by **the devil** (the "chief rabbi" of the synagogue of Satan?). There they would be persecuted for **ten days.** Numbers in Revelation are normally symbolic. We have already encountered seven churches, seven lampstands, and seven angels. The number seven will be repeated many times in Revelation and regularly symbolizes completeness. Other numbers occurring rather frequently are four, ten, and one thousand. Ten days represents a short period of time and is perhaps related in some comparative way to the thousand-year millennium of chapter 20. The advice for this time of trial (suffering is a form of testing) is to **be faithful, even to the point of death.** Those who

8

endure will receive the **crown of life** — that is, the victor's wreath, which is life.

Following the exhortation to hear, the overcomer is promised immunity against the **second death.** In chapter 20 the second death is equated with the lake of fire (v. 14b). To remain faithful during persecution is to overcome, and Christ promises eternal life to overcomers.

12-13 Because Pergamum was the provincial capital of Asia, it had been granted by Rome the "right of the sword" (the authority to take life at will). To this particular congregation, then, Christ is the one who has the **sharp, double-edged sword** (see 11:16). The ultimate power of life and death belongs not to Roman magistrates, but to God.

Reference to the throne of Satan reflects the fact that Pergamum had become the official center in Asia for emperor worship. Satan ruled from Rome in the West and from Pergamum in the East. Yet believers in this citadel of paganism had remained faithful to Christ, even though one of their number, **Antipas,** had been martyred for his faithful witness. (Legend has it that he was roasted to death in a brazen bull.)

14-16 Pergamum, however, was not without fault. Some of its members held to the **teaching of Balaam.** From the book of Numbers (25:1ff. and 31:16), we learn that Balaam had led Israel into apostasy by capitalizing on the seductive activity of Midianite women.

Like the ancient Israelites, some at Pergamum had been enticed into taking part in pagan feasts and the accompanying immorality. Balaam stands as a symbol of all false teachers who urge compromise with the lax standards of the world. The **Nicolaitans** are probably the same group under another name.

Christ admonishes the church at Pergamum to **repent** of its indifference to this heretical development. Pergamum's weakness is the opposite of the one in Ephesus, that is, the jealous guarding of doctrine at the expense of love. Failure to take action will result in a divine visitation of judgment against the offenders.

17 To the overcomer Christ promises **hidden manna** and a **white stone** inscribed with a new name. Manna was the food supplied by God to the Israelites during their long journey from Egypt to the promised land. Hidden manna refers to the heavenly, messianic banquet that awaits all God's people at the end of this age.

The white stone could be an allusion to the ancient custom of using tessera (little tablets of wood, stone, or metal) for a variety of purposes. Here it would serve as a token for admission to the heavenly banquet. The **new name,** known only to the one who receives it, is the name of each faithful believer.

18-19 To the Thyatiran church Christ presents himself as the Son of God with **eyes** like **blazing fire** and **feet** like **burnished brass.** Some writers see an intentional contrast with Apollo, the guardian deity of Thyatira. It is a way of saying that Christ, not Apollo, is the true Son of God. His piercing gaze can see through the cunning arguments of Jezebel. He stands strong and able to carry out his judgment.

Before giving a lengthy reprimand for error, Christ acknowledges the church's **love and faith, service and persever-ance.** The latter grow out of, and are an expression of, the former. Unlike the Ephesian church, which forsook its first love and was admonished to "do the things [it] did at first" (2:5), the Thyatirans were **now doing more than [they] did at first.**

20-25 As at Pergamum, there were those at Thyatira who held to the teaching of Balaam. A certain woman associated with the congregation was encouraging believers to compromise their commitment to God. John identifies her with the name of her Old Testament counterpart, **Jezebel.** That wicked queen of Ahab had encouraged the Israelites into idolatrous worship of the Canaanite Baal (1 Kings 16:29ff.; 2 Kings 9:30ff.). The Thyatiran Jezebel had likewise persuaded some of the local congregation to compromise with the cult by taking part in its religious feasts and **sexual immorality.** She may have reasoned that in a city noted for its many trade guilds (which were inseparably involved with cultic ceremonies), it would be economic suicide to reject the minimum requirements for sect membership. Since "we know that an idol is nothing at all" (1 Cor. 8:4), what harm could come from agreeing to their simple requests? That she claimed the gift of prophecy and had convinced others of this suggests that she was a woman of prominence and possessed considerable persuasive power.

This New Testament Jezebel had been given **time to repent** of her adulterous relationship with the pagan culture, but had refused to do so. Consequently, she is to be cast into a **bed of suffering,** and her paramours are to suffer intensely unless they repent. From 1 Corinthians 11:27-30, we learn that sickness and even death were held to result from spiritual offenses. Jezebel's **children** were all who embraced her doctrine. The judgment of God will fall upon them all, and then the churches throughout Asia will understand that Christ really does search the heart and mind, dealing every man according to his works. The doctrine of judgment based on works is taught in both the Old and New Testaments (see Jer. 17:10; Matt. 16:27; Rom. 2:6).

Those at Thyatira who have not been taken in by Jezebel are admonished to **hold on to what [they] have** until Christ comes. No other burden will be placed upon them. These are they who have not learned **Satan's so-called deep secrets.** This phrase is sometimes taken as a satirical response to the sect's claim of knowing the deep things of God. Or it could be a reference to the Gnostic boast that only by entering into Satan's realm (in this case, by eating at his sacred feast and indulging one's sexual appetites) can the Christian emerge victorious and demonstrate complete freedom from Satan's power.

11

26-29   The overcomer, he who does Christ's will to the end, is promised **authority over the nations.** This promise of ruling the nations is a way of saying that in the new age, which is about to break, the tables will be turned. The Christian minority will no longer be under pressure from Roman authorities, but the righteous will rule over the wicked. Ruling with a rod of iron (the Greek verb means "to shepherd") in this context refers to the shepherd's wielding of an iron-tipped club or staff to ward off preying beasts. The power of secular authority is to be shattered like a broken vessel of clay. The overcomer will also receive the **morning star** — an allusion, perhaps, to the era of eternal righteousness about to dawn.

Revelation 3

To the church at Sardis, Christ presents himself as the one **who holds the seven spirits of God and the seven stars.** In the first verse of chapter 2 we learned that "holding the seven stars" indicated Christ's sovereign control over the churches. That he now holds the seven spirits of God means that his sovereign control extends to heavenly beings. Coupling the seven spirits and the seven stars points to a relationship that exists between the churches and the heavenly realm. All creation exists within the jurisdiction of God.

1-3 Christ is fully aware of all that is going on in the church at Sardis (**"I know your deeds"**) but unfortunately can find nothing to commend. The congregation has the reputation of **being alive**, but in fact it is **dead.** It would appear that the members have so completely come to terms with their pagan environment that there is no longer anything about them to offend anyone. They exist rather comfortably as a Christian church (in name, at least), but in reality are spiritually dead. **Wake up** while there is still hope, exhorts Christ.

The secular history of Sardis provides an interesting parallel to the spiritual condition of the church within its walls. The acropolis was situated on a spur of Mount Tmolus and accessible only from the southern side. On the other three sides, the sheer rock cliffs dropped some 1,500 feet to the valley below.

It was a natural citadel, essentially unassailable. Yet twice in its history the enemy had scaled the walls and captured the city. A false sense of security led to lack of vigilance. In a spiritual sense as well, the church had grown lax. Unless they awake immediately and shore up their defenses, they will fall to the enemy.

Once again memory is summoned as an aid to renewal. The church is to **hear, obey,** and **repent.** If not, Christ will appear as suddenly as a thief. Like the daring Cretan who scaled the cliffs with fifteen men to open the gates and allow the armies of Antiochus to capture the fort, Christ will appear suddenly in judgment.

4-6 Yet even in the complacent church of Sardis, there were some who had not **soiled their clothes.** They are to **walk** with Christ **in white.** In context, soiling one's clothes would refer to defiling involvement with the local, pagan religious practices. White clothes speak of justification. The few who have not sullied their faith by compromise will walk with Christ in the pure garments of righteousness. To **overcome** is to remain true, and that is what keeps one's name in **the book of life.** In Exodus 32:32-33, Moses pled with God for the wayward Israelites, saying that he wished to be blotted out "of the book you have written" if the people's sins were not forgiven. The idea of a divine register was common in Jewish thought. Exactly what it means in the New Testament to be blotted out of this book of life is not clear. The various answers proposed by those who would bring the verse into conformity with a doctrine of "eternal security" are not especially persuasive. Better to let the warning stand as it is, recognizing that phrases taken from a highly symbolic writing provide an inadequate basis for doctrine.

A third promise to the overcomer is that Christ will **acknowledge his name** before God and the angels. During his earthly ministry, Jesus had promised his followers that if they acknowledged him before men, he would acknowledge them before the Father (Matt. 10:32).

7-10 Philadelphia was the city of brotherly love. It took its name from Attalus II Philadelphus, a Pergamene king who earned the title "lover of his brother" by his legendary devotion to his older brother Eumenes II. Philadelphia and Smyrna are the only two churches that receive unqualified praise from Christ. To the Philadelphians, Christ writes as the true Messiah, who exercises absolute control over entrance to the eternal Kingdom. In both the Old and New Testaments, God is called the Holy One (see Isa. 40:25; John 6:69).

The **key of David** stands for complete control over the royal household. Whatever is opened or shut by the person who holds the key cannot be changed. Christ has placed before the church an **open door.** This is often taken to indicate a fresh opportunity for missionary activity. A different interpretation fits the context better. The congregation is a small one (**you have little strength**) but has remained faithful in spite of Jewish opposition. These adversaries are labeled **liars** and their place of worship is called the **synagogue of Satan.** They would undoubtedly have excommunicated any of their group who confessed Jesus as Messiah. Never mind, says Christ. Although the synagogue door has been shut in your face, the door to the eternal Kingdom of God has been opened wide for you. No one can shut that door! The time will come when those who have put you out of the synagogue will acknowledge that you are the ones loved by the Messiah. Verse 9 does not envision the cringing response of defeated enemies. To **fall down at [someone's] feet** is an Oriental metaphor used here to depict the vindication of the church and its faith.

A time of great testing will come to **those who live on the earth.** The reference here and elsewhere in Revelation (6:10; 8:13; 11:10; 13:8; 17:8) is to the enemies of the church. This **hour of trial** is the three-and-a-half-year rule of Antichrist (13:5-10), which precedes the triumphal return of Christ to establish his eternal Kingdom. Since the church had endured patiently the hardships of life in Philadelphia, Christ promises to keep them from the final testing that is to fall upon the enemies of God. Some take this as a promise that Christ will come in some preliminary way to remove the church prior to the difficulties of the last days. Such a "rapture," however, is not specifically mentioned in Revelation. It is better to understand the phrase as a promise that in the final period of demonic assault upon the earth, believers will receive spiritual protection against the forces of evil. This is consistent with Jesus' words in John 17:15, "My prayer is not that you take them out of the world but that you protect them from the evil one."

11-13 The time of Christ's return is not far off (see 1:1; 22:7, 12, 20). **"Hold on to what you have,"** Christ warns, so that no one will take your victor's wreath. As an overcomer you will be placed like a **pillar,** securely and permanently, in the temple of God. To the citizen of Philadelphia, a city that was devastated by the famous earthquake of A.D. 17, the idea of permanence would be especially appealing. The overcomer will also be inscribed with three names: the name of **God** indicates divine ownership; the name of God's **city,** the New Jerusalem, speaks of citizenship in the heavenly commonwealth; and Christ's **new name** suggests the full revelation of his character at the Second Coming. While present problems test the patience of believers, the future is bright and the rewards of faithfulness beyond compare.

14-18 We now come to the last of the seven churches, the church of Laodicea. The passage is well known because of its reference to lukewarmness and its invitation to open the door of the heart and allow Christ to enter (v. 20).

To the Laodiceans Christ writes as **the Amen.** The title is an affirmation of the trustworthiness of Christ, perhaps in contrast to the lack of faithfulness on the part of the church. Since Jesus was **faithful and true** to his witness, he now rules God's creation.

16

The basic fault of the Laodicea church is that it is **lukewarm.** This has been understood to mean that spiritually the church was neither hot nor cold, but had settled for an insipid lukewarmness. It is regularly noted that several miles to the north of Laodicea, the hot mineral water from springs in Hieropolis spills over the cliff above the Lycus River and covers the wide escarpment with a layer of white mineral. By the time the water reaches the spillway, it has become lukewarm and is nauseous to the taste. The problem with this interpretation is the difficulty in understanding why it is better to be spiritually cold than lukewarm.

The real contrast appears to be between the medicinal waters of Hieropolis, which would provide healing, and the cool drinking water of Colossae, ten miles on up the Lycus glen, which would provide refreshment. The Laodiceans were lukewarm in the sense that their Christianity provided neither healing for the spiritually sick nor refreshment for those who were spiritually weary. Thus they were offensive to God. He was about to vomit (the Greek verb is stronger than the NIV's **spit)** them out of his mouth. In their self-sufficiency they viewed themselves as wealthy while in fact they were **wretched, pitiful, poor, blind, and naked.** They were devoid of any realistic understanding of their true condition.

It has often been noted that Laodicea prided itself on its financial wealth (it rebuilt after a major earthquake without help from Rome), an extensive textile industry (its soft, black wool was internationally famous), and a popular eye salve (developed in connection with a renowned medical school). This is undoubtedly the background for Christ's admonition that they buy **gold** from him to become rich, **white clothes** to cover their nakedness, and **salve** to restore their sight. The areas of life that give them smug satisfaction are the very areas in which they need the greatest help!

19-20 One of the fundamental principles of divine training is that love sometimes expresses itself in rebuke and discipline (the Greek word means "to train as a child"). The proper response to divine correction is to **be earnest, and repent.** When God corrects, he takes his stand at the door of the heart and knocks. We must take the next step and open to him. When we respond, and only then, he enters and fellowship is restored and deepened. At no time does God force himself upon the believer.

Verse 20 is often used in evangelism to portray God's desire to enter the heart of the unbeliever and bring salvation. It may be applied in this way, but its primary reference is to believers whose lukewarmness provides neither healing for the sick nor refreshment for the weary. The verse is Christ's corrective message to the self-sufficient believer who, unfortunately, appears unable to recognize his own poverty, shame, and blindness.

21-22   The promise that the overcomer will **sit with [Christ] on [his] throne** is entirely eschatological. It belongs to the coming age. Jesus had promised his followers that in the age to come they would sit on twelve thrones, judging the tribes of Israel (Matt. 19:28).

In Revelation 6:10, the martyrs under the altar will ask how long it will be until their deaths will be avenged. In chapter 20:4-6, the martyrs are raised to rule with Christ for a thousand years. While the images of Revelation are not to be pressed unduly, the scene predicted in the closing verses of the letter to Laodicea is one of universal recognition of the validity of the faith of God's people and the benefits that will follow.

Revelation 4

The seven letters to the churches of Asia are now complete. All seven are to be sent to each congregation along with an account of the visions to follow.

1 John looks up from his scroll, and there before him stands a door opening into heaven. The voice like a trumpet, which had interrupted his meditation in the previous chapter, now invites him up to heaven to learn how God will bring history to a close and usher in the eternal state. In the chapters that follow, we will learn of the events that will take place at the close of history, as well as of the activity of God (and Satan) that lies behind the events.

Some writers hold that the heavenly summons is to be interpreted symbolically as the rapture of the church. Nothing in the verse, however, supports this interpretation. Its purpose is rather to show John what must soon take place so that he can report it to the churches (see 1:11; 1:1-2) — hardly necessary if the churches are to be taken from the earth before it all comes to pass.

2-4 Immediately John is **in the Spirit** and beholds a throne room in heaven. The phrase describes a trancelike state appropriate for the visionary experiences to come. Prophetic ecstasy was not uncommon in Jewish literature (see 1 Kings 22:19; cf.

Acts 10:9-16). It is significant that the first thing John sees in heaven is a **throne.** This symbol, found more than forty times in Revelation, symbolizes power and authority. To churches about to enter a time of persecution, it was important to emphasize that God continues to be absolutely sovereign over the affairs of men and nations. It is God, not Satan, who is writing the final chapter of history.

God himself is not described in the passage. All we know is that on the throne sits One whose brilliance is like the light reflected from precious stones (Paul wrote that God "lives in unapproachable light" and is unseen; 1 Tim. 6:16).

Around the throne are twenty-four other thrones, upon which are seated **twenty-four elders.** Their identity has been widely debated. The view that they represent the entire people of God (the twelve patriarchs of the Old Testament and the twelve apostles of the New) is based upon inferior Greek manuscripts that alter the song of the elders in chapter 5:9-10 to read "purchased *us* . . . made *us* to be . . . *we* will reign." The better manuscripts have the pronouns in the third person, not the first, and read, "purchased *men*," "made *them*," and "*they* will reign." Since in chapter 5 the elders sing of the people of God as a different group, they themselves can hardly be identified as that group in chapter 4. Most likely the elders are an order of exalted angelic beings who worship and serve God in the heavenly throne room.

5-6a Before the throne are seven blazing lamps, which John identifies as the **seven spirits of God** (see 1:4). These also are angelic beings. In front of the throne stretches what appears to be a sea of crystal-clear glass. Rather than attaching a symbolic meaning to each item of the vision, it is better to understand the descriptive details as supporting the overall impression. A **sea of glass** reflecting the brilliance of an emerald-colored rainbow around the throne would heighten the sense of God's transcendence and majesty. **Lightning** and **thunder** recall the appearance of God on Mount Sinai (Exod. 19:16) and appear regularly in similar scenes throughout Revelation (8:5; 11:19; 16:18).

6b-8 Between the throne and the circle of elders are **four living creatures.** Once again we are probably dealing with an angelic order. They are **covered with eyes,** which speaks of unceasing vigilance. Nothing escapes their notice. The first creature resembles a **lion,** the second an **ox,** the third has a face like a **man,** and the fourth is like an **eagle** in flight.

Reference is often made to the four cherubim of Ezekiel (1:5-6, 10), each of which had four faces (lion on the right, ox on the left, human in front, and eagle behind). The similarities and dissimilarities of the two passages illustrate how figures and symbols from the Old Testament are normally altered when they enter into John's vision. Just as a dream frequently employs people and places known to the dreamer (usually with rather dramatic juxtapositions), so John's visions build upon his familiarity with Jewish literature (the Old Testament and non-canonical materials).

It has been suggested that the four living creatures symbolize the entire animate creation. That they take the form of various animals supports this conjecture. Yet their role as leaders in worship (4:9-10; 5:15) seems to assign to them a higher level of significance.

The description continues, noting that each of the four creatures had six wings and was **covered with eyes** (even **under [the] wings**). Since the eyes are referred to more than once (vv. 6 and 8), we may assume that what they represent is especially important. The many eyes indicate that the living creatures are acutely aware of all that takes place in the throne room. They are the guardians of the throne of God. Any attempt to visualize the four creatures by taking the description in a strictly literal sense results in an exceedingly bizarre configuration. This should remind us to concentrate on what the descriptions symbolize rather than on the symbols themselves.

21

The living creatures are angelic beings who surround the throne and take part in unceasing worship of God. **Day and night** they proclaim the holiness of God, the one whose might exceeds that of all others and who not only **is**, but **was**, and **is to come.** To be caught up in adoration of God — the sovereign over all creation, seated upon the throne of the universe — is to enter into the exaltation of the living creatures. The truth is dynamic and existential, not static and intellectual.

9-11 Whenever the living creatures praise and adore the one seated on the heavenly throne, the twenty-four elders prostrate themselves before the throne and worship God, who lives **for ever and ever.** These acts of spontaneous worship in no way contradict the ceaseless praise of verse 8. Revelation is written in a literary style that disregards the rigid expectations of un-imaginative prose.

In verse 8, the living creatures praised God for *who he is.* The twenty-four elders now declare him worthy of honor on the basis of *what he did.* He is **worthy** because he **created all things.** Elsewhere in John's writings there are allusions to a heretical group known as Gnostics, who held that God as spirit could have nothing to do with matter, which was intrinsically evil (see 1 John 4:1-3). The song of the elders corrects the dualistic idea that spirit and matter are essential opposites. God, who is spirit (John 4:24), created everything that is. It was his will to bring all things into existence.

Revelation 5

John's attention is now drawn to a scroll in the right hand of God. In ancient days scrolls were made by joining uniform sections of papyrus (the fibrous inner bark of a plant found in marshy areas along the Mediterranean) and rolling them onto a spindle. Normally they had writing only on the inside, where the fibers ran horizontally. That the scroll in the hand of God had writing on both front and back (v. 1) would suggest the size and completeness of the message it contained.

1 The scroll was sealed with **seven seals** to guarantee that absolutely no one would be able to open it and discover what it contained. Years before, the prophet Daniel was told to "close up and seal the words of the scroll until the time of the end" (Dan. 12:4). Now, however, the end is rapidly approaching and the time has arrived to open the scroll and reveal its contents.

2-4 But now a problem arises. **Who is worthy** to open the scroll and disclose the denouement of history? An angel proclaims the challenge in a **loud voice** so that all can hear. But **no one in heaven or on earth or under the earth** is able to break the seals. This threefold division is not intended to teach a three-tiered universe. Rather, it is a literary figure stressing the universality of the proclamation (see Phil. 2:10 for a similar rhetorical division).

When no one is found worthy to open the scroll, John breaks out weeping. John does not weep because he is personally disappointed that he will not learn how history will turn out, but because, unless the seals are broken, the end will be indefinitely postponed.

5 At this point one of the elders speaks to John and tells him not to weep. There is one who has triumphed and is able to loose the seals and open the scroll. That person is **"the Lion of the tribe of Judah, the Root of David."** Both titles are taken from the Old Testament and were interpreted messianically as referring to the coming Messiah. In Genesis 49, Jacob, in his final blessing upon his twelve sons, calls Judah "a lion's cub" and promises him authority "until he comes to whom it belongs" (vv. 9-10).

Centuries later Isaiah promises a "shoot . . . from the stump of Jesse," an ideal king from the line of David, who will bring to pass an era of peace (Isa. 11:1). Thus it is the Messiah himself who alone is worthy to break the seals and set in motion the final chapter of history. He is worthy because he has **triumphed.** His triumph, as we will learn in verses 9 and 10, is victory through the sacrifice of himself.

6 John now sees a Lamb with seven horns and seven eyes, standing in the midst of the elders and the living creatures. The Lamb looks **as if it had been slain.** Many commentators associate this figure with the sacrificial lamb of Jewish ritual. John the Baptist declared, "Look, the Lamb of God, who takes away the sin of the world!" (John 1:29).

However, several considerations point in another direction. The Greek word used here for lamb *(arnion)* occurs twenty-nine times in Revelation and only once elsewhere in the New Testament. In verses like John 1:29, the more common word for lamb *(amnos)* is used. This suggests a different meaning for the word "lamb" as it is used in Revelation.

Far from being a meek animal led to the slaughter (as in Isa. 53:7), the Lamb of Revelation wages a victorious war over his enemies, overcoming them "because he is Lord of lords and King of kings" (17:14). In the last days the mighty of the earth will call out in desperation to be hidden from "the wrath of the Lamb" (6:16). In Jewish apocalyptic literature, the lamb was used as a symbol for a powerful military leader. Jesus, as the Lamb of Revelation, is the one who will return in the final encounter and lead his people triumphantly to a place of eternal safety (see 19:11-21). His **seven horns** speak of perfect power and his **seven eyes** of perfect knowledge.

7-8 The Lamb steps forward and takes the scroll from the right hand of God. At this moment the angelic hosts fall before the Lamb in worship and praise. From verse 9 on to the end of the chapter we find a magnificent series of hymns of adoration. Each of the elders has a harp and golden bowls full of incense. The **harps** are to accompany the songs about to be sung. The **golden bowls** of incense are the **prayers of the saints.** (This is the second place in Revelation where the author interprets his symbolism; the first is 1:20.) The prayers of God's children ascend to the heavenly throne as a fragrant incense.

9-10 The elders raise their voices in a **new song.** In chapter 4 they gave praise to God for his work in creation (v. 11). Now they sing their praise to the Lamb for his work of redemption. In both cases the exclamation, **You are worthy,** reflects the customary adulation of the emperor as he passed by in triumphal procession.

The Lamb is worthy to open the scroll for three reasons: he was **slain,** he **purchased men for God,** and he granted them the authority to **reign on the earth.** In this context he is declared worthy, not because of inherent worth or any display of personal power, but because he gave himself in death for the redemption of man. His victory led him to death. His exaltation followed his surrender (compare Phil. 2:8-9). It was by means of his death that the Lamb purchased men for God (see 1 Cor. 6:19-20). The scope of his transaction was universal, including people from every nation, tribe, and ethnic group. These are the "other sheep" of whom Jesus spoke in John 10:16.

In the Old Testament the Israelites had been promised that God would make them "a kingdom of priests" (Exod. 19:6). That promise is now fulfilled in the church, the eschatological Israel. Its priestly role is to serve God and **reign on the earth.** At the present time believers share in directing the course of human affairs through prayer. In the future they will reign with Christ (see the millennial scene in chapter 20).

11-12 John now sees a great host of angels round about the throne of God and its inner circle of elders and living creatures. **Ten thousand times ten thousand** is not a multiplication problem but a poetic phrase meaning "beyond calculation." The enormous angelic host raise their voices in an anthem of praise to the Lamb who was slain. He is worthy to receive **power, wealth, wisdom, strength, honor, glory,** and **praise.** He has passed through the dark valley of self-sacrifice and died to redeem "men for God" (v. 9). Now in his exaltation, he is to be adorned with those very attributes which he so willingly laid aside.

13-14 Verse 13 is the culmination of the entire scene of heavenly adoration. Every creature everywhere (that is the meaning of **in heaven and on earth and under the earth and on the sea**) joins in giving praise and honor to God and to the Lamb. The acclamation is so great that it fills the universe. Verse 14 may be understood to indicate that the four living creatures responded with an **Amen** after each of the seven attributes proclaimed by the angelic multitude (v. 12) and each of the four attributes declared by the entire created universe (v. 13). As a fitting finale the elders fall prostrate before the throne and worship both God and the Lamb.

Revelation 6

1-2 The stage is now set and the eschatological drama is about to begin. John watches as the Lamb himself opens the first of the seven seals. With a voice like thunder, one of the four living creatures calls out, **"Come!"** Suddenly a white horse bursts upon the scene. The rider holds a bow and is given a crown. He rides forth as **a conqueror bent on conquest**.

Many scholars take the rider on the white horse to be Christ. In chapter 19 we will encounter another white horse and rider. In that setting there is no question as to the identity of the rider — he is the "KING OF KINGS AND LORD OF LORDS" (19:16; see also 19:13).

When the two passages are studied side by side, however, it becomes apparent that the two riders have very little in common beyond the color of the horses they ride. Since the three horsemen to follow represent the natural consequences of human sin and aggression (red stands for bloodshed, black for famine, and pale for death), it is better to take our clue from **he rode out as a conqueror bent on conquest** and interpret the white horse as the spirit of military conquest. This retains the close relationship between the four horsemen. The interpretation is further strengthened by the fact that in the Old Testament the **bow** was a symbol for military power (see Hos. 1:5) and in the New Testament the **crown** (Greek *stephanos*, "victor's wreath") portrays victory.

3-4 With the opening of each of the first four seals, the same sequence of events takes place — the Lamb removes the seal and one of the living creatures calls for a horse and rider to come forth. The horse that comes out when the second seal is opened is **fiery red** in color. Its rider is given **power to take peace from the earth** and cause men to kill one another. This symbolizes the bloodshed that inevitably follows the passion to conquer (which was symbolized by the white horse and rider). While modern warfare is far more lethal in its destructive power, ancient wars were normally more bloody due to person-to-person combat.

Some writers have suggested that if the white horse represents military aggression from without, the red horse may symbolize internal strife and revolution (**men slay each other**). In the thirty-year period before Herod the Great, over 100,000 people died in revolutions in Palestine alone. The short **sword** (Greek *machaira*, in contrast to *rhomphaia*, "large sword," in v. 8) was well suited to this sort of rebellion.

Note that the rider **was given** power to incite the nations to war. God allows the hostility of men, but he also determines its limits. The strong sense of divine sovereignty running throughout the book of Revelation is the basis for our confidence that God will in fact bring about the final victory of righteousness over evil.

5-6 The third horse to be unleashed is black. Its rider holds a pair of scales in his hand. The **black horse** represents famine. In ancient days, conquering armies lived off the produce of the lands they had just taken. As a result, whatever was left behind would be exceedingly scarce. The **scales** picture the careful weighing out of grain during a time of famine. The voice John hears says that for a day's wages a man is to receive only enough wheat (**a quart**) for himself or enough of the less nutritious barley (**three quarts**) for a very small family.

The prohibition against damaging the **oil and the wine**

28

has been interpreted in various ways. The most satisfactory interpretation is that of a limitation set upon the extent of the famine. Since the roots of both the olive tree and the grapevine go deep into the soil, a drought that would devastate the grain would not necessarily affect the oil and wine. God allows the famine but limits its scope and intensity.

7-8 The fourth horse is **pale** in color (like a corpse or the face of a person struck with terror). Its rider is **Death,** and **Hades** is his inseparable companion. To them is given the power to kill with what the prophet Ezekiel calls his "four dreadful judgments" — sword, famine, wild beasts, and plague (see Ezek. 14:21). These plagues for the most part overlap with the consequences of the previous horseman. In a war in which the fallen would be left unattended, death by wild beasts would be expected.

The four horsemen of the Apocalypse symbolize a kind of limited and preliminary judgment that results from the aggressive nature of man. War and its aftermath are allowed by God as a natural result of man's sin. It is not the direct outpouring of divine wrath. Not until the seventh seal is removed and the scroll is actually opened do we enter into the final stage of judgment that releases the righteous retribution of God upon all the evil of the world.

9-10 Revelation contains three series of plagues — the seals, the trumpets, and the bowls. Each series is numbered one through seven. Each is divided into a set of four (and there are similarities between the sets), followed by an additional three. Thus, after the four horsemen the sequence changes. With the opening of the fifth seal, we find a group of martyrs calling out for judgment upon the wicked and vindication of their faith.

The altar in John's vision seems to be in heaven. The **martyrs** are those whose lives have been sacrificed because of the testimony they have maintained. That they are **under the altar** may reflect the Old Testament practice of pouring sacrificial blood at the base of the altar (see Lev. 4:7). Like Antipas of Pergamum (2:13), they remained true even at the cost of their lives.

The martyrs' plea for judgment upon **the inhabitants of the earth** (a designation for mankind in its hostility to God) should not be taken in the sense of personal revenge. Throughout the Old Testament, especially in the Psalms, there is a profound concern for the reputation and honor of God. For God's people to suffer shame is for God to appear powerless against his enemies. Hence the concern that the faithful be vindicated so that God's name will not be held in dishonor. Since God is **sovereign, holy,** and **true,** he must of necessity avenge the death of the faithful. The only question is when.

11 Each martyr is given a **white robe** symbolizing the righteousness that now belongs to him. They are to **wait a little longer** until the complete number of fellow martyrs is reached. When all who are to sacrifice their lives because of their Christian testimony have been put to death, God will bring history to a close and vindicate the martyrs in final judgment.

12-14 When the **sixth seal** is opened, the entire universe is thrown into turmoil. Not only does a great earthquake alter the face of the earth (**every mountain and island was removed from its place**), but sun and moon are darkened and stars fall to the earth. To the ancients, who viewed the orderly universe as an indication of God's sovereign control, these great cataclysmic events would be a grim announcement that the end had come. In the Old Testament, the earthquake often announced a divine visitation. When God came down on Mount Sinai, "the whole mountain trembled violently" (Exod. 19:18; see also Isa. 2:19).

Since apocalyptic writing is characterized by vivid images and striking figures of speech, this portrayal of a universe in dissolution should not be interpreted with a rigid literalism. The language is similar to the poetic descriptions in the Old

Testament of the mountains skipping like lambs (Ps. 114:4) and the trees of the field clapping their hands (Isa. 55:12). But neither should the passage be allegorized to the point where it represents nothing more than upheavals in the social and political world. It is an apocalyptic portrayal of the end of history, when this world as we know it gives way to eternity.

15-17 The description continues with a dramatic portrayal of how the cosmic upheavals affect mankind. **Kings, princes, generals, the rich** and **the mighty, slave** and **free** — all flee to caves in the mountains. Yet even there security eludes them. Rather than face the wrath of the Lamb, they cry out to the mountains and rocks to fall on them. With the approach of the end and the realization that they are about to face the wrath of God, their hearts are gripped by terror. The rocks and mountains that move at God's command cannot provide a hiding place. Those who have spurned the love of God must now reap his intense hatred of all that is evil and contrary to his holy will. The concept of a wrathful lamb is not paradoxical when we remember that the lamb in Revelation is primarily a messianic warrior, not a meek sacrificial animal.

The sixth seal has brought us to the beginning of the end. In one sense it goes beyond itself and portrays a setting described more fully in the initial trumpets and the first four bowls. Some writers find a repetition or recapitulation in the three numbered series. Close examination, however, reveals not a carefully designed scheme of recapitulation but the free use of common apocalyptic symbols. As the end approaches, there is an accompanying increase in the intensity of distress. Revelation is not prewritten, historical narrative but a highly impressionistic portrayal of the end of the age, the return of Christ, the judgment of evil, and the eternal blessedness of the righteous.

Revelation 7

Chapter 7 consists of two visions that serve as an interlude between the first six seals in chapter 6 and the seventh seal in chapter 8. A similar interlude is found between the sixth and seventh trumpets (10:1–11:13). The strategic placement of these parenthetical sections creates a sense of heightened expectancy as the drama of the last days moves toward its climax.

1 Verses 1 through 8 describe the sealing of the 144,000. John sees four angels standing at the four corners of the earth, restraining the four winds of destruction. The description is highly metaphorical. Reference to the **four corners of the earth** is not intended to imply that the earth is square (or rectangular). We still speak of the "four corners" of the earth. This part of the vision shows that the destructive winds of nature (for instance, the sirocco, a searing wind from the desert that leaves withered vegetation in its wake) are being restrained by heavenly beings.

2-3 Then, **from the east** (perhaps a reference to Palestine), comes another angel bearing the **seal of the living God.** He orders the four restraining angels not to harm the land, sea, or trees until the servants of God are sealed on their foreheads.

The **seal** is probably to be taken as the signet ring used by ancient dignitaries to protect the contents of official documents.

Scrolls were sealed with a small disk of molten wax into which the distinctive seal of the sender was pressed. From Revelation 14:1 we learn that the mark upon the forehead of God's servants consisted of the names of the Lamb and of God the Father. The purpose of sealing the 144,000 is to protect the last generation of believers, who are about to enter the final tumultuous days before the end. The protection is not physical (the two witnesses in chapter 11 are killed by the beast) but spiritual. God insures that the final demonic assault of Satan will be unable to affect the destiny of his people.

It is worth noting that it is the **seal of the living God.** Over against the false and impotent gods of heathendom, the God of the Apocalypse is living and therefore able to grant perfect protection to those who bear his name.

4-8 John does not witness the sealing; he only hears that 144,000 have been sealed. From each of the twelve tribes of Israel 12,000 are sealed. But who in fact are the **144,000**?

Answers abound. Some think that they constitute a select group of martyrs. Yet according to chapter 13:15 all (rather than a chosen few) who do not worship the image of the beast are killed. The careful listing of 12,000 from each tribe suggests completeness rather than selectivity.

Others feel that the 144,000 are literal Jews chosen from the various tribes of a reconstituted nation of Israel. Apart from the obvious historical problem that the ten northern tribes disappeared in Assyria and the other two tribes lost their national identity with the fall of Jerusalem, several irregularities exist in the list as we find it in Revelation. It is **Judah,** rather than Reuben (the oldest son of Jacob), who heads the list. Both **Joseph** and his son **Manasseh** are listed, although the latter would be included with his father. And we would expect Manasseh's brother Ephraim to be listed if the tribe of Joseph is to be divided. Finally, the tribe of **Dan** is omitted.

These irregularities warn us against taking the list as a

33

prophetic genealogical chart. The order in which the tribes are listed is without significance. The number 144,000 is symbolic: it squares the number of tribes of Israel (12 × 12 = 144) and multiplies the sum by 1,000. This is a graphic way of representing the number of faithful believers who will enter the dark days before the end.

They are sealed to identify them as belonging to God and to protect them from the wrath of Satan. Reference to the church as the tribes of Israel comes from the New Testament teaching that the church is the "Israel of God" (Gal. 6:16; cf. Matt. 19:28; Jas. 1:1; 1 Pet. 2:9).

9-10 The two visions of chapter 7 stand in sharp contrast to one another. In the first, John sees 144,000 about to enter the period of secular opposition prior to the end. In the second, we meet an innumerable multitude "who have come out of the great tribulation" (v. 14) and surround the throne of heaven, praising God and the Lamb. The purpose of the second vision is to draw back the curtain of eternity and bring encouragement to believers by revealing the blessedness that awaits them in the eternal state.

The **great multitude** around the throne includes people from every sector of the human race. Every **nation, tribe, people and language** is represented. Their **white robes** speak of righteousness, and the **palm branches** they hold mark the occasion as one of festive joy. Their song is a joyful proclamation that their deliverance has been effected by God and the Lamb. It was the will of God that they be saved, and this salvation was carried out through the death of the Lamb (see 5:9).

11-12 Around the innumerable multitude of saints circles an equally great host of angels (see 5:11). They fall on their faces in worship of God and join their voices in a sevenfold doxology. During his earthly ministry Jesus said that "there is rejoicing in the presence of the angels of God over one sinner who repents"

(Luke 15:10). Imagine the scene in heaven when all repentant sinners stand redeemed before the throne of God!

The first **"Amen"** of verse 12 may be a response to the praise of the multitude in verse 10. Or it may, with the second "Amen," bracket the angels' own doxology. **Praise, glory, wisdom, thanks, honor, power,** and **strength** all belong to God forever and ever. To acknowledge his worth is the privilege of the angelic hosts.

13-14 At this point one of the elders asks John about the white-robed multitude. Who are they and where did they come from? John answers, **"Sir, you know"** (see Zech. 4:5 for the same question-and-answer format to introduce the explanation of a vision). The elder then indicates that the multitude are those **who have come out of the great tribulation.**

Throughout history the people of God have often suffered for their faith. "In this world you will have trouble," promised Jesus (John 16:33). "Everyone who wants to live a godly life in Christ Jesus will be persecuted," taught Paul (2 Tim. 3:12). This continuing antagonism against believers will reach its highest pitch in that final period of turmoil before the end. It will thus become the great tribulation.

The multitude before the throne have **washed their robes and made them white in the blood of the Lamb.** The garments of all men have been stained with sin (see Rom. 3:23). They can be cleansed only by an active faith in the redeeming power of the death of Christ. In John's language, they are washed white in the blood of the Lamb (see Isa. 1:18). The act of washing is not a meritorious act on the part of man — something he does to earn forgiveness. It is a way of portraying faith.

15-17 Since the innumerable host has remained faithful in the period of final testing, they are now rewarded by being in the presence of God and ready to serve him unceasingly. God, in turn, spreads his **tent** over them to shelter and protect them

35

from all harm. This imagery would remind John's readers of the tabernacle in the wilderness and of God's protection of Israel by means of a pillar of cloud by day and of fire by night (Exod. 13:21-22).

Never again will they **hunger** or **thirst**. Beyond the obvious physical reference is the promise that their deepest longings for spiritual wholeness will be satisfied in the eternal state. To a people fully aware of the scorching heat of the Near East, the promise of relief from the sun would be most welcome.

The white-robed multitude is pictured as a flock of sheep with the infinite good fortune of having the Lamb as their **shepherd** (see John 10:1-30). This metaphor reaches back into Old Testament times. The psalmist sang, "The LORD is my shepherd, I shall lack nothing" (Ps. 23:1), and Isaiah said of God, "He tends his flock like a shepherd" (Isa. 40:11). Specifically, the Lamb will **lead them to springs of living water.** Eternal refreshment is in store for those who follow Christ. **And God will wipe away every tear from their eyes.** There will be no sorrow in heaven — only tears left over from the travail of life on earth. These God will quickly remove.

Verses 15 through 17 look forward to that time of eternal joy which awaits the church when it has passed through the great tribulation. This description of heavenly comfort and joy is perhaps the greatest portrayal of eternal bliss to be found anywhere in religious literature.

Revelation 8

The parenthetical visions of chapter 7 are over. The Lamb now resumes his role as the one who opens the seven-sealed scroll.

1 When the Lamb removes the **seventh** and last **seal,** we would expect one great final cosmic catastrophe as the appropriate climax to the series of plagues that began with conquest and war and have increased in intensity as they progressed. Instead, there is **silence.** No sound is heard in heaven for about **half an hour.** Is it not true that silence is often more dramatic than sound! As a prelude to all that is about to follow, it is entirely apropos in this setting.

2-5 The activity described in verses 2 through 5 apparently takes place during the half hour of silence. John sees seven angels standing before God. Each is given a **trumpet.** The trumpet was used extensively in Old Testament times for a variety of purposes. For example, it served to gather the people of Israel (Num. 10:2-3), to celebrate sacred feasts (Num. 10:10), and in connection with the coronation of kings (1 Kings 1:34). In Revelation, however, the trumpets announce the wrath of God. The first four trumpet blasts herald physical calamities, the next two bring demonic plagues, and the last proclaims the demise of all worldly systems.

Scholars are divided regarding the relationship that exists

between the three series of numbered visions (seals, trumpets, and bowls). One view is that they follow each other in chronological sequence, with the last member in each series becoming the sevenfold series that follows. That is, the seven trumpets make up the seventh seal, and the seven bowls make up the seventh trumpet. Since the seven bowls are all contained within the seventh trumpet and the seven trumpets are all part of the seventh seal, it may be said that the series of plagues yet to come belong to the seventh seal. Diagrammed, they would look like this:

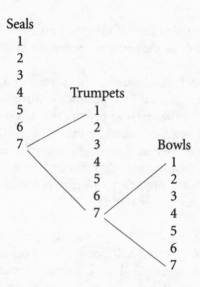

A second approach is called recapitulation. In this scheme, the three series are chronologically parallel, and each brings us to the close of history. The same ground is covered by each series.

Seals	1 2 3 4 5 6 7
Trumpets	1 2 3 4 5 6 7
Bowls	1 2 3 4 5 6 7

My position is that neither scheme is totally accurate. From a strictly literary standpoint, the first approach represents the progression of the text. The recapitulation approach answers the question raised by the close parallelism between the first four trumpets and the first four bowls (plagues fall on earth, sea, rivers and streams, sun, moon, and stars — compare 8:7-12 with 16:2-8). While the numbered visions present a rather clear literary progression, it is less certain that we are to understand a corresponding chronological development. What is clear is that as the end approaches the intensity of the plagues increases correspondingly.

Now another angel approaches the altar. In his hand is a **golden censer** (or fire pan). The **incense** he burns before the altar is mingled with believers' prayers, which ascend to God. (Some hold that the incense *is* the prayers of the saints.) God is mindful of the prayers of his children, which arise unceasingly before the heavenly throne.

The censer, an implement of ceremonial worship, is now put to a different use. It is filled with **fire from the altar** and is **hurled on the earth.** It would appear that prayer has moved God to act in judgment. The prayers of the martyrs in chapter 6 are now beginning to be answered. The angel's hurling fire upon the earth is accompanied by **lightning, thunder,** and an **earthquake** — common symbols of the divine presence (see Exod. 19:16–20:21).

6-9 Against this background, the seven angels prepare to sound their trumpets. At the sound of the **first trumpet,** hail and fire mixed with blood are hurled upon the earth. It is characteristic of John to draw his imagery from existing sources. Both the Old Testament and intertestamental apocalyptic literature supply his rhetorical needs. For example, in Exodus 9:23-25, God rained hail and flashing fire upon the land of Egypt. In the Sibylline Oracles (a collection of Jewish and Christian prophetic utterances claiming to have originated with

39

Greek sibyls or fortune tellers), one of the signs of the last days is a rain of fire and blood. The author of Revelation, however, is not bound by his sources. With sovereign freedom he blends together a kaleidoscope of images, in order to portray a message that bears no essential relationship to the original contexts of its literary sources. Of course, these are still images that John saw. Although God was responsible for the visions, they find expression in the specific terms of John's own religious culture and vocabulary.

As a result of the fire, **a third of the earth was burned up,** as were a **third of the trees** and **all the green grass.** While the first four seals portrayed the inevitable consequences of human sin, the trumpets introduce direct divine intervention in judgment. Yet this judgment is not complete. Always it is one-third of everything that is affected (the fraction occurs twelve times in verses 7-12). From chapter 9:20-21 we infer that the trumpets are warnings intended to call men to repentance.

When the **second angel** sounds his trumpet, something like a blazing mountain is thrown into the sea. **A third of the sea turns into blood,** and a third of the sea creatures and ships are destroyed. Some writers note that less than twenty years before John wrote Revelation, Vesuvius erupted and buried Pompeii in molten lava. It is impossible to determine whether this cataclysm provided the imagery for John's burning mountain. The destruction is serious (one-third) but not complete.

10-12   At the command of the **third trumpet,** a blazing star falls on a third of the rivers and streams, turning them bitter and bringing about the death of many people. Even more terrifying are the results of the **fourth trumpet.** Blackness settles over the earth for a third of the day and a third of the night. Sun, moon, and stars are blackened.

Do not try to press these details into some sort of prosaic scheme. As the trumpets are sounded one by one, God begins to disrupt the orderly processes of nature as a warning and

40

prelude to the greater disaster about to come. Cosmic disturbances such as hail, bloody fire, blazing mountains, falling stars,
and darkness are warnings intended to move the wicked to
repentance.

In the first-century world, they would strike terror to the
heart of man. But even terror will not deter man from his
idolatry and shameful life (see 9:20-21). Neither God's kindness
(Rom. 2:4) nor his severity is able to alter the conduct of man
in rebellion against God. His destiny is determined by his willful
resistance to all divine overtures.

13   The seven trumpets are divided into groups of four and
three (as with the four horsemen of 6:1-8 and the three seals
that follow). The first four trumpets call forth plagues upon
nature, which affect man indirectly. The remaining plagues are
demonic forces, falling directly upon man. They are introduced
by a bird of prey, either an **eagle** or a vulture, hovering overhead
and screeching, **"Woe! Woe! Woe to the inhabitants of the
earth."**

The plagues that follow do not fall upon the church but
upon the pagan world. In chapter 9 the scorpions are to harm
"only those people who do not have the seal of God on their
foreheads" (9:4). Although believers in the last days will suffer
the abuse of the wicked (as they always have — see John 16:33;
2 Tim. 3:12), they will never be subject to the wrath of God.

Only if tribulation is defined as the direct outpouring of
God's wrath could it be said that the church is kept from going
through the tribulation. The church always was and always will
be (until the Second Coming) subject to the hostility of the
world. The final stages of that opposition is what we designate
as the tribulation.

Revelation 9

It took only six verses for John to describe the first four trumpet plagues. Now he devotes an entire chapter to the next two plagues. This indicates the seriousness of the woes that are yet to come.

1-6   At the sound of the **fifth** trumpet, a star falls to the earth. The **star** is obviously a person, because the text goes on to say that *he* takes a key and opens the abyss. Out billow dense clouds of smoke blotting out the sun and darkening the sky. The **Abyss** is a great subterranean chasm inhabited by all kinds of evil beings — the scorpion centaurs who torture men, their demonic King Abaddon (v. 11), and the cruel beast of chapter 11 who assaults and murders the two witnesses.

The **locusts,** swarming out of the abyss and emerging from the smoke, are given the scorpion's power to torture but not to kill. In the Old Testament, the locust served as a symbol of devastation and destruction. The prophet Joel pictured the dark side of the coming day of the Lord by means of a great plague of locusts (Joel 1:2–2:11).

The demonic locusts of Revelation, however, do not harm the vegetation. Rather, they inflict their torture upon those inhabitants of the land who do not bear **the seal of God on their foreheads.** This is strong evidence that believers will never be abandoned to the evil powers of the underworld. They may

42

be buffeted by man, but they are sealed against demonic powers (see Rev. 7:1-8; also the protection given the children of Israel from the first Egyptian plagues, Exod. 8:22; 9:4, 26; etc.).

The locusts are allowed to torment man for a period of **five months.** This period of time may stem from the life expectancy of the locust. It represents a limited period of torment during which man may still repent of his wickedness (vv. 20-21). In one of the most vivid presentations of human distress, we learn that during those days **men will seek death, but will not find it;** they will **long to die, but death will elude them.** The issues at stake in the age-long conflict between God and Satan are deadly serious. To choose wickedness is a decision that leads to unmitigated suffering.

7-12   The locusts are described as **horses prepared for battle.** The similarity between the head of a locust and a horse's head has often been noticed. In fact, the German word for locust is *Heupferd* (hay horse). The description of the demonic locusts is bizarre in the extreme. Their **faces** are like human faces. They wear **something like crowns of gold.** They are covered with long **hair** like that of a woman, and their **teeth** are like a lion's. The picture that emerges combines human intelligence and animal cruelty. It is unnatural and frightening.

The locusts are protected by **breastplates of iron.** Their flight sounds like a multitude of chariots rushing into battle. One of the nonbiblical Jewish books tells of elephants that wore coats of mail and made a terrific din as they charged the enemy. As we learned earlier, the locusts have scorpionlike tails and the power to inflict pain for five months.

They also have a king. His name in Hebrew is **Abaddon,** the destroyer. In case the reader fails to grasp the significance of the Hebrew name, John adds the Greek equivalent, **Apollyon.** As king of the demonic locusts, his mission is to destroy. Some find here a cryptic reference to the practice of certain Roman emperors who regarded themselves as an incarnation of the god

Apollo. The play on words (Apollyon/Apollo) would be a subtle way of saying that the emperor of Rome was in fact the king of the underworld and all its destructive forces.

Commentators who understand the bulk of Revelation as describing life in the present age normally interpret the locusts as a personification of evil. Hair "like women's hair" is said to symbolize the seductive nature of evil. But hairy locusts with lions' teeth and scorpions' tails are not most people's idea of a seductive creature! Although certain features in this portrayal may represent truths that have found expression from time to time in human history, I believe the locust plague is an eschatological event. It belongs to the end of time. The last three trumpet plagues are called the three woes. Verse 12 announces that the terrifying horde of demonic locusts is only the first woe. Two more will follow. The plight of the unrepentant will continue from bad to worse as the end approaches.

13-19 When the **sixth angel** blows his trumpet, John hears a **voice** from the **golden altar.** It is helpful to remember that the martyrs in chapter 6 who called out for vindication were "under the altar" (v. 9). Further, the prayers of the saints in chapter 8 rose from "the golden altar before the throne" (v. 3). The point is that the prayers of God's children play an active role in bringing about the close of history. In Jesus' sermon on the last days, he indicated that the end will come only after the gospel of the Kingdom of God has been preached throughout the entire world (Matt. 24:14).

The voice from the altar orders the sixth angel to release **the four angels who are bound at the great river Euphrates.** The Euphrates was the longest river in western Asia (almost 1,800 miles) and, following the conquests of David, marked the eastern boundary of Israel (2 Sam. 8:3; 1 Kings 4:24).

The four angels are apparently in charge of the demonic cavalry that is about to ride across the earth, killing a third of mankind. (The word "angel" is often used in secular sources for supernatural beings connected with the underworld.) They have been **kept ready** for this specific moment in time. Note the emphasis on year, month, day, and hour. God is in control and will release the forces of destruction when he decides the time is exactly right.

The mission of the locusts was to torment (v. 5). The mission of the cavalry is to **kill** (v. 15). As each new plague brings man closer to the end, the intensity of punishment increases. Apparently even the severest of plagues fails to move man to repentance (vv. 20-21). The mounted troops released by the four angels are beyond calculation. The figure **two hundred million** is not to be taken as an actual number. The Greek says, "a double-myriad of myriads." We might translate, "countless thousands" (a myriad is 10,000). What we need to sense is how absolutely terrifying the sight would be. It would instantly paralyze even the bravest with fear and demoralize all potential opposition. All we are told about the riders is that they wear multicolored breastplates. They do not play an active role in carrying out the plague. The colors (**fiery red, dark blue,** and **yellow**) match the fire, smoke, and sulfur that come from the mouths of the horses.

The horses are grotesque. They have lionlike heads with mouths that breathe out fire and smoke. Their tails are like snakes with heads that inflict injury. Picture an enormous cavalry of fire-breathing monsters sweeping over the land. Add to it their demonic origin and their power to kill, and you will sense the terrifying reality of the second woe. The great horde moves relentlessly across the face of earth, leaving a third of mankind dead.

20-21 The final verses of chapter 9 are a sad commentary on human nature. One would think that a plague of demonic horses killing one out of every three persons would bring the survivors to their senses. But those who were not killed in the three plagues of fire, smoke, and sulfur **did not repent** of their idolatry. They continued to worship demons and dumb idols they had crafted of wood, metal, and stone. Further, they did not repent of their heathen practices of murder, sorcery, immorality, and theft. When people turn willfully from the knowledge of God, they quickly pass the point of no return and continue without delay along the road leading to idolatry and immorality (see Rom. 1:18-32).

The theme of idolatry is prominent in Jewish literature. Not until the seventy years of Babylonian captivity did the Israelites overcome their persistent tendency to lapse into pagan worship. On Mount Carmel, for instance, the prophet Elijah laid out the options for Israel: "If the LORD is God, follow him; but if Baal is God, follow him" (1 Kings 18:21). In the New Testament Paul taught that to offer sacrifice to an idol was to sacrifice to demons (1 Cor. 10:20). At the end of time, men will still choose to honor and worship the demons that inflict suffering and death. Such is the perverse nature of those who refuse to acknowledge the lordship of Christ.

It is interesting to note that three of the four vices listed in the final verse of chapter 9 are specifically prohibited in the Ten Commandments. The second (magic arts, or witchcraft) is listed by Paul as a work of the flesh (Gal. 5:20), which ultimately leads to the fiery lake of burning sulfur (Rev. 21:8).

Revelation 10

Between the sixth and seventh seal there was an interlude consisting of two related visions (7:1-8, 9-17). We now encounter a similar parenthesis between the sixth and seventh trumpet (10:1–11:14). From a literary standpoint, the interludes are dramatic pauses that heighten the sense of expectancy as the end draws near. In addition, the two visions that follow the sixth trumpet will answer the questions "How long until the end?" and "What will happen to the church during this troubled period?"

1-4 At the beginning of chapter 4, John was summoned from earth to heaven. It was from that perspective that he saw the visions that followed. Now he is once again on earth (he sees an angel **coming down from heaven**). The mighty angel who descends is described in Old Testament terms. In Psalm 104:3, God is said to make the clouds his chariot. The rainbow was a sign of his covenant with man that the earth would never again be destroyed by water (Gen. 9:8-17). When Moses came from the presence of God on Mount Sinai, his face shone with such radiance that he had to wear a veil (Exod. 34:29-35).

In Revelation, the angel's **legs like fiery pillars** would recall the pillars of fire and cloud that guided (Exod. 13:21-22) and gave protection (Exod. 14:19-24) to the children of Israel as they fled from the armies of Pharaoh during the Exodus.

I mention these Old Testament parallels only to point out that visions, like dreams, draw from the wide range of knowledge and experience that has gradually become a part of the writer himself. In the same way that Paul's writing reflects a vocabulary and style different from Luke's (yet it is God who speaks through both), so the visions of John are cast in terminology and images that were dominant in his spiritual growth and background.

The mighty angel plants one **foot on the sea** and the other **on the land.** This stance is probably intended to emphasize the tremendous size of the angel, although some scholars find here a reference to universal sovereignty. In his hand is a **little scroll.** In contrast to the seven-sealed scroll of chapter 4 whose content could be known only after each seal was removed, the little scroll **lay open** to be read without delay.

The angel gives a great shout like the roar of a lion, and the **seven thunders** respond. Exactly who the seven thunders are is not known. Nor is there any indication of what they said. All we know is that John was about to write down what he heard when he was told by a voice from heaven to **"seal up what the seven thunders** had **said"** and not record it. Some interpreters think that the thunders may have given another series of warning plagues, but since man had not repented after the extreme distress caused by the earlier plagues, there would be no reason to go through yet another series. Obviously this is conjecture, but it is not inconsistent with what we might have expected.

One additional point needs to be made. When the seven thunders spoke, John was going to write down what they said. It appears that during his visionary experiences the apostle kept notes, which later made up a large part of the book of Revelation. This accounts for the vivid descriptions that characterize the book. Revelation is not the literary product of an exiled eccentric bent on creating an exciting drama but the eyewitness account of a prophet who was in the Spirit (1:10; 4:2) and described what he actually saw.

5-7 The mighty angel who stood astride the land and sea **raised his right hand to heaven** and swore by the one who lives forever that the end of this age would take place without further delay. In ancient days (as well as today) raising the right hand was part of taking an oath. In Deuteronomy, God himself is pictured as lifting his hand to heaven and swearing that he will take vengeance on his enemies (Deut. 32:40).

The description of God as the one **who lives for ever and ever** would be an encouragement to early Christians facing the likelihood of martyrdom. Man may take life, but God is beyond the threat of death and supplies eternal life to the faithful. He is also the Creator. As the one who created all things out of nothing (Heb. 11:3), he is able to carry through what he began.

Human beings have always been interested in the question of how long it will be until the end. There have been those in every generation who were convinced that they were living in the last few moments of history. There was a widespread expectation among followers of a certain popular spokesman that Christ would return on or about September 24, 1988. Numerous believers dressed themselves in white and spent the day on the top of a hill or a mountain. As the end seems to draw near, concern for its actual arrival increases. The martyrs under the fifth seal asked, "How long, Sovereign Lord . . . until you judge the inhabitants of the earth and avenge our blood?" (6:10).

The immediate answer had been to wait (6:11), but now the mighty angel can declare, **"There will be more delay!"** The warning plagues have gone out and man has refused to repent. Whatever was intended by the seven thunders has been canceled. From this point forward, nothing can stop the inexorable flow of events that will bring history to its close. All restraint is to be removed, and man will enter the final dark hours of Satan's great wrath (12:12, 17).

During the period of time introduced by the trumpet blast of the seventh angel, the **mystery of God** is to be brought to completion. A mystery in biblical thought is a truth that was formerly hidden but is now made clear by revelation. Mysteries often have an eschatological coloring. For instance, the mystery of 1 Corinthians 15:51-52 (a change from mortality to immortality) takes place when Christ returns. The mystery of God that is to be accomplished in the day of the seventh trumpet is the completion of God's great redemptive mission, purposed in creation and made possible by the work of the Lamb (5:9-10). Note that God has determined the overthrow of evil from the very first. His purpose to redeem runs throughout history. He announced it to his prophets. As Amos wrote, "Surely the Sovereign LORD does nothing without revealing his plan to his servants the prophets" (Amos 3:7).

8-11 Once again the voice from heaven speaks. John is told to **take the scroll** from the hand of the angel. Remember that the angel was robed in a cloud with a rainbow above his head, his face was like the sun, and his legs were like fiery pillars. Besides that he was standing over both land and sea (v. 1). Nothing short of a command from heaven could make John approach such a supernatural colossus and deliberately remove a scroll from his hand.

But John obeys the heavenly voice and takes the scroll. He is then told to **eat it.** What follows in the text is presented in the form of a riddle. The scroll will be as **sweet as honey** in the mouth but will turn the stomach **sour.** John eats the scroll and finds this to be true. But what are we to make of this strange experience?

To eat the scroll means to digest thoroughly its contents. The psalmist wrote that God's words were sweet to his taste, "sweeter than honey" to his mouth (Ps. 119:103). Jeremiah reports that upon finding God's words, he "ate them," and they became the delight of his heart (Jer. 15:16).

Writers differ regarding what constitutes the little scroll and what it means. My opinion is that it is a message for the believing church and that it makes up the first thirteen verses of the following chapter (11:1-13). In this latter section we will learn that after the witnessing church has completed its testimony, the Christians will be put to death. As the great scroll of chapter 5 dealt with the destiny of all mankind, the little scroll reveals the lot of the faithful during the final period of Satanic opposition. The scroll is sweet to the taste because there will be no more delay in bringing to a close God's eternal purpose to redeem mankind. It will be sour in the stomach because it will involve a time of fierce opposition and much sorrow.

In verse 11 John is told that he must **prophesy again** about the destiny of mankind as a whole. In the seals and the trumpets, we learned of judgments against the ungodly. After the interlude of 10:1–11:14 (the church in the world during the final days) John will return to the theme of God's judgment of the wicked (11:15ff.).

There is a sense of divine compulsion in the fact that John must prophesy again. His task is not over until he has carried it through to the very end. There is much that remains before Satan and his emissaries are put away forever and righteousness dwells in a renovated heaven and earth. Until the revelation is complete, John must continue to prophesy.

Revelation 11

The first thirteen verses of chapter 11 constitute the message of the little scroll that was sweet in the mouth but sour in the stomach. They deal with the fate of the witnessing church during the final period of hostility just before the end. Obviously, the little scroll needs to be interpreted symbolically. If we interpret symbols in a literal fashion we misinterpret the intended meaning.

Furthermore, a great number of words operate on several levels of meaning. The Alamo was a Franciscan mission at San Antonio, but in the slogan "Remember the Alamo" we are not expected to recall the physical construction of the fort. We are to remember the courage of the small band of Texans who held out bravely against the larger number of Mexican troops but in the end were massacred. In this context "Alamo" is to be understood as a symbol of bravery in battle.

It is crucial to remember that wherever the context calls for interpretation on a symbolic level, a literalistic interpretation inevitably involves misrepresentation. Literalness must never be automatically equated with accuracy or truthfulness. For instance, in the section that follows we will discover that the temple is not a building but the New Testament church.

1-2 John is given a reed and told to measure the temple of God but not the outer court. He is to count the worshipers. The outer court is to be left unmeasured because it has been given over to the Gentiles, who will trample on the holy city for forty-two months. What does all this mean?

The **temple** is the church, the people of God (see 1 Cor. 3:16-17; Eph. 2:19-22). To **measure the temple** means to preserve it. God's people are to be protected in the coming catastrophe (compare the sealing of the faithful in 7:1-8).

Yet the outer court is to be trampled underfoot. In another sense the church is to be subject to severe opposition and suffering. How do these two ideas fit together? In the last days the church will suffer persecution, but it will be provided spiritual sanctuary against the assaults of Satan. Its protection is against spiritual danger, not physical. Martyrdom has always been a potential hazard of following Christ in a godless world, but Satan cannot harm spiritually those who have made a genuine commitment to Christ.

The **42 months** during which the holy city (the church) is trampled underfoot by pagan forces corresponds to the 1,260 days of 11:3 and 12:6 and to the "time, times and half a time" (three and a half years) of 12:14. The background for this time period seems to be the three and a half years during which the Jews suffered under the Syrian tyrant Antiochus Epiphanes (167-164 B.C.). It had become symbolic for a limited period of unrestrained evil.

3-6 We now meet the **two witnesses.** Like the four horsemen of chapter 6 and the 144,000 of chapter 5, the identity of the two witnesses has long intrigued New Testament scholars. While we may not be able to identify them with absolute certainty, we are able to understand their mission and destiny.

The two witnesses are dressed in **sackcloth** (the garment of mourning and penitence; see Matt. 11:21). Anyone who would harm them is devoured by fire coming from their mouths. They can **shut up the sky** so that it will not rain; they can **turn the waters into blood** and **strike the earth with every**

kind of plague as often as they wish. They exercise this authority during the time of their prophesying — 1,260 days or forty-two months (solar months have thirty days).

As I understand Revelation, the two witnesses represent the church in the last days before the end. They are modeled after Moses, who turned water to blood (Exod. 7:14-18) and smote the earth with every plague (Exod. 7–11), and Elijah, who consumed his enemies with fire (2 Kings 1:10-12) and kept the heavens from raining (1 Kings 17:1). It was a common Jewish expectation that Moses and Elijah would return before the end of the age (Mal. 4:5; John 6:14; Deut. 8:15). Like these two great leaders of Israel, the New Testament church is to proclaim its message with boldness until the very end. God will see to it that nothing silences the witnessing church until its mission is accomplished.

The two witnesses are also identified as the **two olive trees** and the **two lampstands** that stand before the Lord. The background for this vision is Zechariah 4. The two olive trees in the Old Testament vision are Joshua the high priest and Zerubbabel the Jewish governor. The people of God combine these two roles. They are a "royal" (Zerubbabel) "priesthood" (Joshua), called to "declare the praises of him who called [them] out of darkness into his wonderful light" (1 Pet. 2:9).

7-10 When the two witnesses have completed their task, they are attacked and killed by the beast of the abyss. This is the first mention of **the beast,** the great persecutor of the church in the last days. We will learn a great deal about this figure in chapters 13 and 17. For the present, note that he **comes up from the Abyss,** the place of demons (see Luke 8:31; Rev. 9:1-11). He is demonic in nature, a powerful ally of Satan. It must also be noted that it is not until the witnesses have completed their mission that the beast is allowed to prevail. Until the very end, God remains in control.

The bodies of the witnesses **lie in the street of the great**

city for three and a half days, during which time the inhabitants of the earth celebrate the death of their tormentors. In eastern lands it was considered a great disgrace to be deprived of a proper burial. We see the church in the last days persecuted and scattered by the world. The world scornfully denies burial to the defeated minority, whose death is cause for great celebration.

The city in which the witnesses lie martyred is **figuratively called Sodom and Egypt** — that is, it is like each of these cities in some way. Sodom symbolizes moral degradation (Gen. 19:4-11), and Egypt stands for oppression and slavery. Elsewhere in Revelation, the **great city** consistently refers to Rome (16:19; 17:18; etc.). Because the clause **where also their Lord was crucified** is added, many commentators have taken the city to be Jerusalem.

John wrote Revelation from the perspective of his own historical setting. Rome was the great enemy of the church. Emperor worship threatened the young congregations scattered throughout the empire. Rome is the beast who would, by its absolute power, force its will on all believers.

But in a fuller sense John writes of the actual consummation of world history that is still future. Rome is not simply an ancient and powerful city. It is also the concentration of brute force that in the last days will launch an all-out attack upon God and his people.

The symbols of Revelation are taken from the first century but will find their complete fulfillment only at the end of time. Thus "the great city" in verse 8 is not simply the Rome of John's day. It is rather the debased sexuality of Sodom and the cruel oppression of Egypt, which characterize the totalitarian regime that will control all mankind at the end of history. It is the eschatological Rome. Since it is the essence of all that is unrighteous, it can also be considered the place where our Lord was crucified.

11-12   After the three and a half days during which the dead bodies of the two witnesses lie exposed, God brings them back to life, and they rise to their feet. One is reminded of Ezekiel's vision of the valley of dry bones, brought to life by the breath of God (Ezek. 37). While the enemies of righteousness stand by struck dumb with terror, a loud voice summons the church to heaven. In full view of an astonished world, the church is taken up into heaven in a cloud. Certainly this is the rapture of the church. And it is no secret!

Although the rapture is pictured in chapter 11, it does not necessarily take place before the events recorded in the next few chapters, which picture believers as still on earth. The book of Revelation is not written sequentially from a temporal point of view, but in the order in which John received the visions. Here he is given an indication of the church's future vindication.

In summary, the account of the two witnesses teaches that the church will carry out its fundamental mission of bearing witness until the very end. The vast majority of men will not repent and believe. When the church's mission is complete, it will appear that Satan has won a total victory over the people of God. But God will intervene and vindicate forever those who have placed their trust in him.

13-14   As the two witnesses are taken up in a cloud, the city is rocked by a violent **earthquake.** A tenth of the city collapses, and 7,000 persons are killed. In Jewish thought, earthquakes were associated with periods of divine visitation. When God came down upon Mount Sinai "the whole mountain trembled violently" (Exod. 19:18). Throughout Revelation earthquakes accompany critical moments of divine activity — in 6:12 when the sixth seal is broken, in 8:5 when the fire from the heavenly altar is cast upon the earth, in 11:19 when the heavenly temple is opened, and in 16:17-18 when the final bowl is poured out.

The survivors of the earthquake are **terrified** and **give**

glory to the God of heaven. This does not mean that they will repent and become believers. It only means that they acknowledge his superior power and might as demonstrated by his control over nature. It does not imply personal trust or a redemptive relationship.

Verse 14 notes that the second woe is now passed and a third is coming soon.

15-18   When the **seventh trumpet** sounds we would expect the third woe (as in 9:1, 13); but instead we hear **loud voices in heaven** proclaiming that all earthly dominion has been transferred to God. It is the long-awaited declaration that God has triumphed over evil and established his eternal reign. While in one sense this act was accomplished on the cross, in another sense it awaits a future manifestation. It is then that every knee shall bow and every tongue confess (Phil. 2:10-11). The church lives in the interim period between the defeat of Satan and his final expulsion. To grasp the certainty of both events is to live victoriously in the present.

The twenty-four elders fall before God, adoring and thanking him for taking his power and entering into his reign. God is the **Almighty.** None can stand before his awesome power. He is the one **who is and who was.** No longer is he the one "who is to come" (see 1:8) because, from a prophetic perspective, he is already here. He has begun his eternal reign. The nations rose in anger, and God has answered with holy **wrath.** The time for final judgment has arrived. This judgment anticipated by the elders will be carried out at the great white throne described in 20:11-15. Those who destroy the earth are to be destroyed. God tailors the punishment to fit the crime.

For the righteous, however, it will be a time of reward. The saints, that is, those who reverence the name of God, whether they be prominent or relatively unknown, will all share in the reward of their faithful commitment to Christ.

19 In response to the elders' hymn of thanksgiving (vv. 17-18), the temple in heaven is opened, revealing **the ark of [God's] covenant.** In the Old Testament, the ark was a sacred chest that symbolized the presence of God with his people. In John's vision, the ark would be a reminder of God's faithfulness in keeping his covenant promises during the difficult days lying ahead. The lightning, thunder, earthquake, and hail are related to the wrath that God is about to pour out on the unrepentant world.

Revelation 12

The three sevenfold series of plagues in Revelation are the seals, the trumpets, and the bowls. When the seven seals were removed, the scroll of destiny was opened to reveal the end of history as it began to draw near. The seven trumpet plagues serve to announce the arrival of the last days and summon men to repentance. Now, just before the third series of plagues (the bowls of God's wrath in chapters 15–16), John is taken behind the scenes of history to learn the fundamental reason for the intense antagonism that is mounting against the church in the last days. To understand that the rising tide of persecution is simply the final death struggle of an already defeated foe will encourage believers to hold fast until the ordeal is over.

1-6 As John's vision opens, there appears in the sky a woman clothed with the sun. The moon is under her feet, and a crown of twelve stars adorns her head. The scene depicts both authority and splendor. The woman is about to give birth to a child.

A second sign appears — a great red dragon with seven heads and ten horns. Upon his heads are royal crowns (the woman's crown is a *stephanos,* "victory wreath," while the dragon's crowns are *diademata,* "royal crowns"). The horns of the dragon symbolize his power. With his enormous tail, he sweeps stars from the sky and hurls them down to earth. The dragon positions himself in front of the woman in order to devour the child the moment it is born.

These figures are not difficult to identify. The **woman** is not Mary the mother of Jesus, but the true Israel through whom Jesus (in terms of his human nature) entered into history (see Rom. 1:3). This interpretation is consistent with the fact that later in the same chapter the woman becomes the church, the "Israel of God" (cf. Gal. 6:16). In the Old Testament, the enemies of Israel are often portrayed as dragons (Ps. 74:14; Isa. 27:1, KJV). John's readers would immediately understand the great **red dragon** to be Satan, the archenemy of God and his people (in verse 9 he is specifically identified as such).

The child to be born is Christ. He is the **male child** destined to rule the world with a rod of iron. The dragon's eagerness to devour the child explains the violent opposition that Jesus met during his earthly ministry. It began with the slaughter of the male children in Bethlehem (Matt. 2:16) and ended on a cross outside the city of Jerusalem.

But Satan's plans are thwarted. The child is **snatched up to God and to his throne** (a reference to the Ascension). When he returns at the end of time, he will **rule all the nations with an iron scepter** (cf. 19:15). This does not refer to a period during which Christ will govern the world with great severity, but, as a shepherd would use his staff to protect his flock from marauding beasts, so will Christ strike down the enemies of righteousness who oppress and persecute his church. The rod of iron speaks of judgment rather than governance.

When the child is taken up to heaven, the woman flees to a desert sanctuary prepared by God. There she remains for **1,260 days,** protected and nourished by God. Her time of protection in the desert corresponds with her time of persecution (cf. 11:2; 13:5). The church needs to know that in the troubled days ahead God will provide a spiritual refuge for believers, enabling them to withstand the violent opposition of Satan.

7-9 John now records a war that takes place in heaven. The combatants are **Michael and his angels,** pitted against the **dragon and his angels.** The forces of righteousness prevail, and the dragon and his defeated army are hurled to the earth. This does not portray the primordial expulsion of Satan from heaven. The scene is eschatological. It enters the narrative to explain the intense hostility the church will experience in the last days. When the devil is cast out of heaven, he "is filled with fury, because he knows that his time is short" (v. 12).

The church must recognize that there is a basic antipathy between God and Satan, right and wrong, believer and unbeliever. James puts it unequivocally, "Friendship with the world is hatred toward God" (Jas. 4:4). Jesus said, "If they persecuted me, they will persecute you also" (John 15:20). In the last days, Satan, who failed in his assault upon heaven, makes war against the offspring of the woman — "those who obey God's commandments and hold to the testimony of Jesus" (v. 17). Behind the scenes of history lie the eternal purpose of God and Satan's opposition to everything it proposes. This insight reveals the root cause of the believer's difficulties and should encourage his endurance under trial.

The dragon is identified in three ways:

(1) He is that **ancient serpent** who leads the whole world astray. The obvious reference is to the historic encounter between Eve and the serpent in the garden of Eden (Gen. 3). Deceit has always been Satan's method. Should he ever tell the truth, his evil intentions would be laid bare.

(2) The dragon is **Satan.** Originally the word "Satan" was not a proper name. It simply meant "adversary." In time it came to stand for *the* adversary, Satan. He is the prosecutor who accuses men in the court of heaven (Job 1:6-12).

(3) The dragon is also called **the devil,** which means "slanderer." By accusation and slander he would lead the whole world astray. Having fallen from heaven, he now desires to take

as many as possible with him into the torments of hell (cf. 20:10, 15).

10-12 Revelation contains a number of passages best described as dramatic outbursts of praise. Verses 10 through 12 furnish one of the finest examples (see 4:8; 7:10; 19:1-2 as well). A loud voice proclaims that the sovereign rule of God has become a reality and with it authority and deliverance.

The great accuser has been hurled from heaven. He no longer enjoys the privilege of a heavenly courtroom in which to level accusations night and day against the brethren (cf. Rom. 8:33-34). He was overcome, not only by the death of the Lamb, but by the faithful testimony of the believing church as well. Satan is now a defeated foe! Expelled from heaven and rendered powerless by the cross, he is helpless against those who are willing to forfeit their lives in faithful obedience.

The defeat of Satan causes great rejoicing in heaven. At the same time it brings woe to earth because the devil has come down, full of fury, knowing that his time is about up. This explains the suffering of the righteous during the last climactic period of history.

13-17 Following the hymn of praise, which interrupted the narrative of Satan's expulsion from heaven (vv. 10-12), John continues the account. The dragon, recognizing his defeat by the hosts of heaven, now directs his hostility toward the woman who gave birth to the male child. The woman is the ideal Israel. Now that Christ has ascended to the throne of God, **the woman** is the New Testament church. This shifting of symbols is common in apocalyptic literature (earlier the woman was the righteous remnant within Judaism). A similar example of fluid imagery is found in Revelation 17:9, where the seven heads of the scarlet beast are not only seven hills but also seven kings.

Satan pursues the woman, but she is given the wings of an eagle and flies off to a place prepared for her in **the desert.**

In Old Testament thought, the desert was held to be a place of divine protection and nurture. For forty years God provided for his people in the wilderness. Hosea told of God luring Israel into the desert in order to speak tenderly to her (Hos. 2:14). The woman is to be kept in the desert out of the serpent's reach for the period of final turmoil, designated **a time, times and half a time** (forty-two months or three and a half years). Her protection is spiritual.

In his zeal to get at the woman, the serpent spews out a great river of water. He would sweep her away, but the earth opens its mouth and swallows the torrent. The scene depicts the intensity of Satanic hatred against the church. Although we are obviously dealing with metaphors (the earth has no **mouth**), the truths they communicate are as real as if they had been phrased in nonmetaphorical language.

The dragon, enraged at this turn of events, goes away to make war against the rest of the woman's offspring, instead of the male child Jesus. Verse 17 defines **the rest of her offspring** as **those who obey God's commandments and hold to the testimony of Jesus.** The nature of apocalyptic language makes it possible for the church to be symbolized both by the woman and by her offspring.

The major point of chapter 12 is that because Satan has been defeated in heavenly battle, he is now going to vent his anger upon God's children on earth.

Revelation 13

The first sentence of chapter 13 belongs to the preceding chapter (it is designated 12:18 in the Greek text). It is the dragon (not John, as the King James Version has it) who stands on the shore of the sea. From that vantage point, the dragon calls forth the first of two great beasts who are to carry out his campaign against the woman's offspring.

1-4   John sees a **beast** emerging from **the sea.** Like his master, the great red dragon, the beast has **ten horns and seven heads** (cf. 12:3). In Revelation, the number seven stands for completeness. A seven-headed beast would signify the ultimate enemy of the church. The **blasphemous names** inscribed on the seven heads reflect the growing tendency within the Roman empire to consider the emperor as a divine being. Domitian (who was emperor at the time of John's visions) wanted to be addressed as "Our Lord and God."

The beast combines characteristics of the **leopard, bear,** and **lion.** It is helpful to note that the prophet Daniel used the same three animals (plus a fourth) to represent four historic kingdoms hostile to the people of God (Dan. 7:3-8, 17, 23). Against this background, John is saying that the beast out of the sea epitomizes all worldly opposition to the Kingdom of God. Of crucial importance is the fact that the power and authority exercised by the beast have been given to him by Satan.

And who is this beast? In John's vision the beast is the Roman empire. It is that concentration of secular power which claims a religious sanction for its cruelty and injustice. Yet the beast is more than the Roman empire. In a larger sense it is the spirit of godless totalitarianism that has energized every authoritarian system devised by man throughout history. At the end of time, the beast will appear in its most malicious form. It will be the ultimate expression of deified secular authority.

John notes that one of the beast's seven heads had received what appears to have been a **fatal wound.** The wound, however, **had been healed.** In chapter 17 an interpreting angel will give us an explanation of the beast and his seven heads (17:8-17). For the moment it is enough to note that the beast possesses remarkable powers of recuperation. He appeared to have been dealt a fatal blow but recovered.

In its long history of abuse and oppression, secular power has often been dealt what seemed to be a fatal blow. Somehow it has always survived. The eschatological beast will bear the mark of this age-long struggle. The whole world will be astonished at the recuperative power of the beast. Men worship the dragon (Satan) because he gives his authority to the state. They worship the state because nothing can match its awesome power or is able to wage a successful war against it. The Roman empire supplied John with the portrait of a cruel and despotic foe. The world has yet to see how terrifying this beast will be in its final incarnation.

5-8 The beast was **given a mouth** (that is, caused to speak) to utter **proud words,** even **blasphemies.** Four times in the Greek text of verses 5 through 7 we read the passive "was given." This phrase emphasizes the subordinate role of the beast. He operates at the bidding of his master, Satan. The time of his delegated authority is **forty-two months** (a span of time well understood by now; cf. 11:2-3; 12:6, 14). A number of phrases throughout this section echo the prophet Daniel (for instance, the little horn of Dan. 7:8 with its "mouth that spoke boastfully").

The beast is a blasphemer. He slanders the **name** of God (that is, the character of God as revealed in his name), his **dwelling place,** and **those who live in heaven.** In 2 Thessalonians 2:4 we have a somewhat parallel passage in which the "man of lawlessness" (the Antichrist) "exalts himself over everything that is called God . . . proclaiming himself to be God."

In John's day the blasphemy of the beast was the increasing tendency to deify the Roman state by granting divine titles to its emperors and erecting temples in which to worship the spirit of Rome. In the last days the secular state will wield extraordinary power and attempt to validate its role by religious sanctions.

Evil disguised as good is the ultimate lie. From recent history we have learned that an entire civilized nation can be led into accepting blatant error as long as the lie is big enough and told often enough. Christians need to stay alert to all the devious and seductive ploys of Satan.

The beast is granted the power **to make war against the saints and to conquer them.** Although overcome physically, the church is yet the victor. In Revelation 15:2 we will read of those in heaven who were "victorious over the beast." True victory for the believer is to remain faithful in the crucial test of faith. The authority given to the beast is exercised over all men everywhere. All the inhabitants of the earth (genuine believers excluded) will worship the beast.

During his earthly ministry Jesus warned of false Christs who would "deceive even the elect — if that were possible" (Matt. 24:24). He himself was tempted to worship secular power (Matt. 4:8-10) — a temptation that in the final days will capture the allegiance of all whose names are not recorded in the Lamb's **book of life.**

The idea of a divine register is common in biblical thought. It is the Lamb's book, for eternal life is possible only because the Lamb was **slain from the creation of the world.** The cross was no afterthought, necessitated by the Jew's rejection of an earthly kingdom. It belongs to the eternal decrees of God. Those who will be faithful in the coming trial have their names recorded in that book of life.

9-10 At this point in the narrative a proverbial saying is introduced to teach that in the coming trial the believer must accept what God has ordained and not counter the state's brutality with force. The saying is composed of two short stanzas, each of which sets up a condition and gives the result. If the believer goes into captivity, then **into captivity he will go.** It is so ordained. If the believer takes up the sword to defend himself (the NIV is different here in that it follows a different Greek textual tradition, which casts the verb into the passive voice), then **with the sword he will be killed.** John adds that this prospect calls for **patient endurance and faithfulness** on the part of the saints.

11-17 We come now to the second beast. As the first beast came "out of the sea" (that is, from across the sea — Rome, to be specific), this beast comes out **of the earth** (from within Asia Minor itself). Elsewhere in Revelation the second beast is called the "false prophet" (16:13; 19:20; 20:10). He is a deceiver. His **two horns like a lamb** suggest gentle persuasion.

In view of his role as a miracle worker who deceives the inhabitants of the earth, it is best to understand the beast's speaking **like a dragon** as a reference to the beguiling speech of the serpent in the garden of Eden. As the first beast exercised the authority of the dragon, the second beast exercises the authority of his immediate superior. The evil trinity is now complete — Satan, the beast, and the false prophet.

Who is the false prophet? In John's vision, the beast was

Rome with its claim to absolute power. The false prophet would symbolize the local priests of Asia Minor who enforced the imperial cult of emperor worship. In the last days the false prophet will represent religious authority bent on making people worship secular power. Even today certain religious groups seem committed to undermining and destroying basic New Testament Christianity.

The role of the false prophet is to make men worship the beast whose fatal wound was healed. In spite of numerous defeats, secular humanism revives and lays claims to man's devotion. In carrying out his task, the false prophet is enabled to perform miracles. Like a new Elijah preparing the way for a new "Messiah," he causes **fire to come down from heaven** (cf. 1 Kings 18:38). Whether or not these are real miracles makes no particular difference as far as our interpretation is concerned (cf. 2 Thess. 2:9). They accomplish their goal of leading men astray.

The false prophet orders the people to erect an **image in honor of the beast.** He then gives breath to the image, causing it to speak. All those who refuse to worship the image are **to be killed.** This demand will effect a clear division between those who are willing to pay the price of their faith and those who would rather capitulate to the Satanic religion of Antichrist. This defection is the great apostasy that precedes the return of Christ (cf. 2 Thess 2:3). Nominal Christians do not forfeit their lives for a cause in which they really do not believe!

Economic boycott is another tactic of the false prophet. Everyone who would buy or sell must have the **mark . . . of the beast** on his right hand or forehead. This mark is the numerical equivalent of the name of the beast. A favorite pastime in ancient days, when letters of the alphabet served as numbers, was to produce a riddle by giving a name in its numerical equivalent. To decipher the name from the number was a challenge.

One famous graffito from Pompeii reads, "I love her whose number is 545." The Jews called the practice *gematria*.

The number of the beast, which was to be placed on the forehead or hand, was 666 (according to v. 18).

18 Verse 18 is the most enigmatic in the book of Revelation. It challenges the reader to identify the beast by working backward from the numerical equivalent of his name. No wonder the verse begins with the assertion, **This calls for wisdom.**

The literature on Revelation is well stocked with proposed answers. Irenaeus (a second-century theologian who lived in Asia Minor) offers such suggestions as "Lateinos" (the Roman empire) and "Teitan" (the Titans of Greek mythology), but admits that the solution escapes him. A commonly held answer is "Nero Caesar," but this has several difficulties as well.

Some writers take **666** in a symbolic sense to indicate a trinity of imperfection. One writer, taking his clue from Revelation 17:11 (in which the beast is said to be an "eighth king"), has discovered that all numbers up through eight when added together equal thirty-six, and that all the numbers up through thirty-six when added together equal 666. Thus 666 would not refer to any certain person; it would simply stand for the beast. If John's intention was to camouflage the identity of the beast, we can only conclude that he was eminently successful! The riddle remains.

Revelation 14

As you read through Revelation you will notice that mingled among the darker scenes of judgment are bright glimpses of the blessedness that awaits the faithful. Chapter 13 served as a grim reminder of the severe testing to which the believer will be subjected. But with chapter 14 we are suddenly lifted up out of the path of the approaching storm and placed with the faithful on Mount Zion. The obvious purpose of the ensuing vision is to provide encouragement for those who refuse to yield to the demands of Satan and his emissaries.

1-5 Once again John sees **the Lamb.** In chapter 5 the Lamb was the only one found worthy to open the scroll of destiny. In chapter 7 he received the worship and praise of the innumerable multitude who emerged from the great tribulation. Now, along with the **144,000,** he stands on **Mount Zion** (that sacred place long associated with divine deliverance). The 144,000 are the faithful who earlier (in chapter 7) were sealed against spiritual harm. In contrast to the inhabitants of the earth (who are branded with the mark of the beast), the 144,000 have the name of the Lamb (and God' s name) on their foreheads. That is to say, they belong to the Lamb.

John hears a great **sound from heaven,** which he describes as the roar of a cataract or the swelling crescendo of a great ensemble of harpists. It is the sound of the 144,000 lifting their

70

voices to sing a **new song** — the anthem of redemption. No one can learn this song except those who have paid the price of endurance and experienced the joy of deliverance. Not even the angelic hosts are able to sing such a song.

The 144,000 are described in three ways:

(1) They are those who did not **defile themselves with women.** Some commentators take this in a literal fashion, holding that it refers to an elite group of saints who had renounced all sexual relationships. Others understand it as describing those who have not become involved in adultery and fornication. I prefer a more metaphorical interpretation. In the Old Testament Israel is often spoken of as a virgin (1 Kings 10:21; Jer. 18:13). Idolatry was portrayed as spiritual harlotry (Hos. 2). Correspondingly, the 144,000 are the bride of Christ who as they await his return have not defiled themselves by lusting after the pagan world system.

(2) They are those who **follow the Lamb.** They walk as he walked. In their daily lives they carry out his commands and follow his teaching.

(3) They are a sacrificial offering to God. Having been purchased by the blood of the Lamb, they offer themselves to God for his purposes. In stark contrast with evil men who love and practice falsehood (22:15), the 144,000 are blameless — no lie is found in their mouths.

6-7 In rather quick sequence, we hear from three angels. The first angel summons mankind to worship the Creator (vv. 6-7), the second announces the downfall of Babylon (Rome) and the great harlot (v. 8), and the third portrays the torment coming upon those who bear the mark of the beast (vv. 9-11).

The first angel flies **in midair** so that all can hear what he is about to say. The **eternal gospel** he proclaims is not the good news of God's redemptive activity in Jesus Christ, but, as the following verse indicates, a call for men to fear and worship God the Creator. The message is for all men everywhere. The hour of judgment has come. To **fear God** is to hold him in reverence; to **give him glory** is to honor him for who he is and all he has done.

This final call to worship is based upon God's action in creation. In Romans 1:18-20, Paul established that men are without excuse because God has revealed himself in creation. It is on the same basis that the angel now makes one last appeal.

8 A **second angel** follows the first and proclaims the fall of **Babylon the Great.** The ancient city of Babylon in Mesopotamia was the political and religious capital of a world empire. It was known for its affluence and moral corruption. In John's day Rome was a contemporary Babylon, symbolizing the spirit of godlessness that draws men away from the worship of God.

Babylon is described as having made the nations **drink the maddening wine of her adulteries.** The picture that emerges is of a prostitute seducing the world with the intoxicating influence of her corrupt practices. This theme is developed fully in chapter 18. Babylon has **fallen** in the sense that God has decreed that it be so. The decree allows it to be prophetically declared as fait accompli. It is interesting that the announcement takes on the wording of the prophet Isaiah in his oracle against ancient Babylon (Isa. 21:9).

9-11 A **third angel** now proclaims the fate of those who choose to worship the beast and bear his mark. They will **drink of the wine of God's fury** and be tormented forever with burning sulfur. The first figure draws upon the Old Testament practice of picturing the wrath of God as a draft of wine (Job 21:20; Ps. 75:8). The wine of God's fury has been poured full strength into the cup of his wrath.

The Bible does not support the notion that divine wrath is nothing more than the consequence of breaking some impersonal laws of nature (for example, obesity is the penalty for overeating). The wrath of God is his righteous response to man's refusal to accept his love. Since sin is personal, so is God's response to sin.

The second figure, **tormented with burning sulfur** (the

Greek says fire and sulfur, or brimstone), reflects God's judgment upon the ancient cities of Sodom and Gomorrah (Gen. 19:24). It is perhaps the most vivid symbol in the New Testament. To suffer forever in a sea of burning sulfur staggers the mind. Many modern writers object to the doctrine of eternal punishment on the basis that it is impossible to reconcile it with Jesus' teaching on love. Yet it was this same Jesus who taught that it would be better to cut off a hand and go through life maimed than to live with two hands and go into hell "where the fire never goes out" (Mark 9:44).

Even if the fire of hell should prove to be no more than an apocalyptic symbol, it still speaks of a terrifying experience of torment and eternal loss. We dare not discard the clear teaching of Scripture on hell because we cannot grasp it fully or because it runs counter to our sensitivities. We should remember that as fallen human beings we have to a great extent lost our awareness of the seriousness of sin.

Those who worshiped the beast (both the pagan world and apostate believers — the latter group is implied in v. 12) are tormented in the presence of the Lamb and his holy angels. Believers had suffered public abuse at the hands of their antagonists; now the tables have been turned, and their oppressors suffer before a heavenly tribunal. There is no rest **day or night. The smoke of their torment** ascends **forever.**

12 The prospect of eternal torment calls for **patient endurance on the part of the saints.** Those who are tempted to relinquish their faith in Christ and agree to join in emperor worship should recognize that such a compromise has fatal and far-reaching consequences. Better to endure the momentary opposition than to yield and find oneself forever cut off from God. **Saints** are simply those who keep God's commandments and remain faithful to Jesus. The great apostasy referred to in 2 Thessalonians 2:3 testifies to the fact that in the final showdown many will be unwilling to pay the price of allegiance to Christ because it will involve physical suffering.

13   John hears a voice from heaven declaring the blessedness of those who **die in the Lord.** Faithfulness may lead to martyrdom, but those who forfeit their lives will be blessed because they will enter victoriously into an eternal rest. This is contrasted to the fate of apostate Christians and those who have never made any pretension of believing. Death for them means eternal fire.

The **rest from . . . labor** that awaits the faithful has nothing to do with normal toil. It is the end of all the trials brought upon believers by the demands of emperor worship. The deeds that **follow them** are acts of resistance to the religious demands of the state. Wherever secular power has camouflaged its unlawful intentions by donning the respectable robes of religion, the result has been flagrant disregard for human rights. At the end of time, the world will witness this unholy alliance in its most monstrous configuration.

14-16   Chapter 14 closes with two related visions of divine judgment. The first (vv. 14-16) pictures judgment as a grain harvest. John sees a reaper **like a son of man** seated on a **cloud** with a golden **crown** on his head and holding a **sharp sickle** in his hand. The reaper is Christ. He awaits the command from the heavenly temple to exercise judgment. The return of the warrior Messiah in chapter 19 will be another presentation of the same great event.

An angel comes out of the temple to tell the reaper to proceed with judgment, because the appointed time has come and the earth is ripe for harvest. The one seated on the cloud swings his sickle, and the earth is harvested. Some writers prefer to interpret verses 14 through 16 as the gathering of the righteous, but it is more consistent with the chapter as a whole to take the unit as a general portrayal of coming judgment.

17-20   The second vision of judgment is pictured as a vintage (the gathering of grapes to be pressed for wine). An angel with a **sharp sickle** steps forth from the temple. A second angel orders him to swing his sickle on the earth and gather the ripe grapes. This second angel comes from the heavenly altar and is in charge of the fire. In 8:3-5, an angel at the golden altar offered incense to God along with the prayers of the saints. If this is the same angel, we may infer that the prayers of the faithful play a definite role in the judgment of the wicked.

The grapes are cut and thrown into **the great winepress of God's wrath.** Any view of God that omits his wrath is defective. Without wrath against sin, the love of God would be no more than maudlin sentimentality. The holiness of God demands his wrath against unrighteousness. While God forgives sin, his righteous character forbids any final acceptance of those who reject his forgiveness.

In ancient days the grape harvest was trampled by foot in a trough. A duct took the juice to a lower basin. To trample grapes was messy business. In the Old Testament, the grape harvest served as a common figure for the wrath of God on his enemies (Isa. 63:3; Joel 3:13).

In the Revelation passage, the grapes are trampled **outside the city.** As Jesus suffered "outside the city gate" (Heb. 13:12), so also will his righteous judgment take place there. As the wine flowed red from the press, so will the blood of the wicked flow from God's great winepress. The quantity of blood is staggering. It rises as **high as the horses' bridles** and sweeps out in a gigantic wave for almost two hundred miles. One person calculated the exact volume of blood and decided that not enough people have lived on earth to supply the demand. Obviously such a computation overlooks the hyperbolic nature of the statement. What it means is that the victory of Christ's return and the ensuing judgment will be absolutely unprecedented.

Revelation 15

In chapter 12 two signs appeared in heaven — the radiant woman and the enormous red dragon. Now a third sign appears — **seven angels with the seven last plagues.** They are the *last plagues* in that they bring to a close God's warning to the impenitent. They do not, however, exhaust the wrath of God, for the lake of fire remains for all whose names are not written in the Lamb's book of life (cf. Rev. 20:15).

1-4 The third series of numbered plagues is about to begin. In verse 7 the seven angels will be given golden bowls filled with the wrath of God. In the chapter to follow (ch. 16) all seven bowls will be poured out upon the earth and its inhabitants. From a literary standpoint, the seven bowls are the unfolding of the seventh trumpet in the same way that the seven trumpets expanded the seventh seal.

The vision of the seven angels with which the chapter begins is interrupted by another vision (vv. 2-4). John sees what appears to be a **sea of glass mixed with fire.** Beside the sea stand those who have emerged **victorious over the beast and his image.** This means that they have remained faithful to God in spite of all the threats and contentious activity of the Antichrist and his henchmen.

The victors are presented harps, and they sing what John calls **the song of Moses . . . and the song of the Lamb.** Exodus

15:1-18 records the song of Moses, which celebrates the Lord's historic deliverance of his people from Egyptian bondage. This deliverance prefigured a greater deliverance that would be achieved by the Lamb. It is on the basis of this great redemptive triumph that the overcomers of Revelation lift their voices in praise to God for who he is and all he has accomplished.

The hymn itself (vv. 3b-4) may have been used in the early church. Practically every phrase reflects the rich vocabulary of the Old Testament (for instance, Ps. 111:2; Deut. 32:4; Mal. 1:11). With its focus on the greatness of God, it serves as a pattern for all other hymnody.

God is the **Almighty.** He is able to accomplish anything and everything he has purposed to do. He is **King of the ages,** and his sovereignty knows no limits. All nations will come to him and worship because he alone is holy and his righteous acts have been made known. This act of universal recognition does not imply the personal salvation of all men. It is a way of stressing the comprehensiveness of God's righteous activity on behalf of man.

5-8   Following the victors' song of praise, John sees that the temple in heaven is opened. The sacred shrine is more closely defined as the **tabernacle** (or tent) **of Testimony** (the portable sanctuary in which God dwelt during Israel's wandering in the wilderness). It is called the tent of Testimony because it contained the two tablets of testimony that Moses brought down from Mount Sinai (Deut. 10:5). In the present context the opening of the tent suggests that the seven last plagues are to come from the presence of God. They come in fulfillment of his covenant relationship with those who have remained faithful.

From the temple emerge the seven angels of destruction. They are dressed in **clean, shining linen** and have **golden sashes** around their chests. This would indicate that the role they are about to play is both priestly and royal. One of the four living creatures (those guardians of the throne in 4:6; 7:11; and 14:3)

hands the angels **bowls filled with the wrath of God.** The reign
of wickedness is almost over. God will vindicate himself. His
wrath will be poured out upon all who refuse his love.

When the angels of destruction receive their bowls of
wrath, the temple is **filled with smoke** (symbolizing the glory
and power of God). God's presence is often accompanied by
smoke (Exod. 19:18; Isa. 6:4). In John's vision the smoke serves
to warn people that no one will be allowed to enter the holy
place until the seven last plagues have been poured out. No one
can approach God until his wrath is complete. The time for
repentance is over. The patience and long-suffering of God have
been exhausted. The doors of access to the presence of God are
closed and judgment has begun.

Revelation 16

Everything is now in readiness for the final series of plagues. The seven angels of destruction have received their bowls of divine wrath. They await the command to pour them out upon all who have made the fateful decision to follow the beast.

There are a number of parallels between the trumpets and the bowls. For example, in each series judgment falls upon the earth, the sea, the inland waters, and the heavenly bodies. This has led some scholars to take the two series as covering the same sequence of events, the difference being a matter of perspective. Such an approach runs counter to the literary structure of the book in which each series is the expansion of the last unit of the previous series. It also overlooks the many differences between the series.

1-3 A **loud voice from the temple** (perhaps the voice of God since the temple is now closed to anyone else; cf. 15:8) orders the seven angels to go and pour out the bowls of God's wrath. The **first angel** carries out his charge, and **ugly and painful sores** break out on everyone who bears the mark of the beast and worships his image.

The bowl judgments share a number of similarities with the ten Egyptian plagues (Exod. 7:14–12:30). For example, the ugly sores of the first bowl are like the boils and abscesses of the sixth Egyptian plague (Exod. 9:9-11). The sea of blood of the second bowl parallels the turning of the Nile into blood (Exod. 7:20-21). While the plagues of Revelation are by no means slavish copies of earlier disasters, they are described in terms that reflect the traditional imagery and vocabulary for such events.

Note that God's wrath falls on those who have declared themselves to be his enemies. God's people are nowhere to be found in this saga of divine judgment. While Christian believers may suffer at the hands of the wicked (not even Jesus, the perfect man, was immune from that), they will never be subjected to the wrath of God poured out in the last days upon the followers of the beast.

The **second angel** pours out his **bowl** on the sea. The translation "bowl" is to be preferred to the King James's "vial" because the Greek word specifies a shallow dish rather than a bottle. The contents of a bowl are quickly and easily poured out!

The second bowl plague turns the sea into **blood like that of a dead man** — that is, coagulated and putrid. *Every* **living thing** in the sea dies. Recall that the second trumpet plague turned *a third* of the sea into blood, and that *a third* of the living creatures in the sea died (8:8-9). The limited consequence of the warning trumpets now gives way to the complete devastation of the bowl plagues.

4-7 The **third** bowl is poured out on the rivers and springs of water. They, too, become blood. Water is absolutely essential for life. God's judgment deprives the wicked of a basic necessity for sustaining life. Death is the final reward for sin.

At this point the angel of the waters declares that God is just in his judgments. Followers of the beast have shed the blood of the righteous; it is therefore entirely appropriate that they should have to drink blood. The punishment fits the crime.

The **angel in charge of the waters** should probably be thought of as a supernatural being connected in some way with the rivers and springs that have just been turned to blood. God is described as the one who is and who was (v. 5). Earlier in Revelation (1:4, 8; 4:8), he was also the one who is to come. This future reference is no longer needed because the final sequence of events is already under way. God has come in judgment.

The altar adds its testimony to the angel's declaration. The judgments of God are **true and just** — that is, they are fully deserved and carried out with fairness. God is addressed both as **Lord** (absolute sovereign) and **Almighty** (nothing lies beyond his power to achieve). He is the ultimate judge of all men, and no one can stay his hand.

8-9   The **fourth angel** pours out his bowl of divine wrath upon the sun. When the fourth trumpet blew, a partial eclipse followed (8:12), but now with the fourth bowl, power is given to the sun to scorch the inhabitants of the earth with an intense heat. (The Greek text reads, "And men were scorched with a great scorching.") One would think that such intense pain would cause people to repent of their evil ways and acknowledge the supremacy and greatness of God. But this is not the case. Instead they **curse the God of heaven** who brought the plagues upon them. Their commitment to evil is so complete that repentance is no longer possible. To serve the beast is to become like the beast!

10-11   The **fifth** bowl is poured out on the throne of the beast, and his kingdom is **plunged into darkness** (compare the ninth Egyptian plague, Exod. 10:21-29). The darkness intensifies the people's distress, and they gnaw their tongues in agony. It is not a pretty picture. Justice demands that the intensity of divine retribution corresponds to the seriousness of rejecting divine love. Men curse God for their pains and sores but refuse to repent. Earlier we read that the beast "opened his mouth to blaspheme God" (13:6). Now his followers, who have taken on the character of their leader, curse (or blaspheme) the name of God. Inevitably, we become like the one to whom we give our allegiance.

12-14 The **sixth angel** of destruction pours out his bowl on the **Euphrates** River. Its waters dry up in order to **prepare the way for the kings of the East.** The Euphrates marked the eastern boundary of the Roman empire. The land beyond the river was controlled by the Parthians, an enemy nation greatly feared by the Romans. For the Euphrates to dry up would symbolize the imminent danger of invasion from without. The kings are gathered for the battle of Armageddon (vv. 14, 16), but after joining forces with the beast (17:12-14) they turn against Rome and destroy her (17:16-18; described in detail in ch. 18).

This destruction of ancient Rome foreshadows the ultimate collapse of all secular power and authority at the end of history. History will not reveal a gradual turning to truth until the entire world is ready to accept the One they once spurned. To the contrary, God will suddenly break in, devastating the opposition and establishing his sovereignty in human affairs.

John sees **three evil spirits** that look like **frogs** coming out of the mouths of the unholy trinity. This evil triumvirate consists of Satan, the beast, and the false prophet (the "beast coming out of the earth" of 13:11-17). The evil spirits are demonic and deceptive. The deceitful quality of evil men is stressed in the New Testament. Jesus warned that in the last days false prophets would lead men astray with signs and wonders (Matt. 24:24). Paul says that the coming of the lawless one will be with counterfeit miracles and deceit (2 Thess. 2:9-10). The specific role of the three demonic spirits in Revelation is to gather the kings of the entire world for battle on the **day of God** (described in 19:11-21). We will learn more of this battle site in a moment.

15 In a short parenthetical statement (v. 15) we are reminded that as the end approaches, believers are to remain alert. The risen Christ reminds the faithful of the unexpectedness of his return — **"Behold, I come like a thief!"** (cf. Matt. 24:42-44; 1 Thess. 5:2). Blessed is the one who stays awake and **keeps his clothes with him.** He will not be caught naked at the return of Christ and be shamefully exposed. The point of the illustration is that the last days will require believers to be vigilant and discerning so that the deceptive propaganda of Satan will not lead them astray.

16 The narrative resumes, and we learn that the three evil spirits gather the kings of the world to a place that bears the Hebrew name **Armageddon.** This cryptic reference has become one of the more widely discussed problems in Revelation. Where and what is Armageddon?

When you examine modern speech translations, you will discover that the designation is often written Har Magedon. Har means "mountain," while Ar (as in the reading Ar-mageddon) is probably "city." Megiddo was an important city that guarded a strategic military road running between the coastal plain near Mount Carmel and the famous valley of Esdraelon. The valley is one of the most famous battlefields in history. Because there is no real mountain (Har) of Megiddo and because the city itself (Ar) does not seem a likely place for massive warfare, many writers have taken the designation symbolically as referring to the final overthrow of the forces of evil by the power of God. Taken in this way, it portrays the victory of righteousness over evil at the close of the age. It is described as warfare in order to depict the conflict and the victory to follow as vividly as possible.

17-21 The **seventh angel** pours his bowl into the air and a voice from the temple declares, **"It is done!"** The seven angels have completed their awesome task. Now follow lightning, thunder, and an earthquake more devastating than man has ever known. The great city (Rome) is split into three parts, and cities around the entire world collapse.

Writers differ about whether or not these physical phenomena should be taken in a literal sense. Will there be actual earthquakes, or is the earthquake a way of saying that every stronghold raised by man against God will be utterly shattered in the coming judgment? The reader who understands the earthquake to be a physical shaking must be careful not to miss the theological significance of the event. The reader who interprets the earthquake as a metaphor of divine intervention must guard against the tendency to consider it as no more than poetry. In both cases something is happening. God has given the great secular enemy of the church (**Babylon the Great,** symbol of luxury, cruelty, and vice) a cup filled with his passionate hatred of evil.

John's vision moves kaleidoscopically. The islands of the sea flee away. Mountains cannot be found. The sky opens and huge hailstones weighing up to a hundred pounds each crash down upon mankind. By this time it is no surprise that even this cataclysmic display is met with resistance on the part of men. Instead of repenting, they curse God for the plague of hail.

Revelation 17

We are about to encounter yet another enemy of God and his people. This time it will be the great licentious whore who sits astride a scarlet beast. She is the royal courtesan of the kings of the earth. Drunk with the blood of saints, she holds in her hand a golden goblet filled with the filth of her obscene profession. In chapter 19 we will meet a radically different female figure — the bride of Christ dressed in "fine linen, bright and clean" (19:8). The contrast is striking!

1-2 One of the seven bowl angels invites John to witness the punishment of the notorious prostitute. As we work our way through chapter 17 we will encounter several important figures who will then be interpreted for us. We will learn that the **woman** is "the great city that rules over the kings of the earth" (v. 18), the **waters** are the people of the world (v. 15), and the **scarlet beast** is the first beast of chapter 13 whose seven heads are "seven hills" and also "seven kings" (vv. 8-9) and whose ten horns are "ten kings who . . . war against the Lamb" (vv. 12-14). While the interpretation that is given helps to identify the harlot and the waters, it is less instructive in its explanation of the beast, as we shall see later.

The Old Testament often speaks of religious apostasy as whoredom. For example, Hosea taught that Israel would be put to public shame because she had played the harlot with

Canaanitish religious practices (see also Isa. 1:21; Jer. 2:24). In Revelation, the harlotry of Rome (the prostitute) is not religious but secular. It has to do with the seductive methods used by that powerful city in gaining control over the entire world. She (that is, Rome) has **committed adultery** with the **kings of the earth.** This means that she has enticed them into compromising relationships. The nations are **intoxicated with the wine of her adulteries.** The supposed benefits of such alliances have made them lightheaded and unable to grasp what is happening.

3-6 John is now carried away in the Spirit to a desert place. There he sees a woman sitting on a scarlet beast with seven heads and ten horns. The beast is covered with **blasphemous names.** By the time Revelation was written, it was not uncommon for a Roman emperor to claim or at least accept a title that implied deity. From the Christian's point of view this blasphemous practice amounted to nothing less than heresy of the worst possible sort. God alone is to be acknowledged as divine. To refer to a secular authority as "Lord" would be to deny to God his unique role as the universal sovereign.

The woman is dressed in the luxurious garments of ancient royalty. Since **purple and scarlet** dyes were expensive to extract, they were used primarily by the very rich. The harlot is said to be **glittering** with ornaments of gold, precious gems, and pearls. The picture is one of wanton luxury and extravagance. Her ostentatious display of wealth testifies to the success of her immoral trade. In her hand she holds a golden cup **filled with abominable things and the filth of her adulteries.** Her cup promises carnal delight, but it is full of the sewage of her sensual practices.

On the harlot's forehead is a mysterious inscription. (Note: the NIV regards **MYSTERY** as part of the inscription). She is **BABYLON THE GREAT, THE MOTHER OF PROSTITUTES AND OF THE ABOMINATIONS OF THE EARTH.** This designation indicates that by John's day, Rome, like her earlier counterpart ancient Babylon, represented the very epit-ome of vice, luxury, and power. She had led all the nations of the earth into her vile trade. Her abominable practices were found everywhere. Not content with her own debauchery, she had infected the entire earth with her lust and disease.

From Roman history we learn of an empress by the name of Messalina who frequently slipped out of the palace at night and served as a whore in a public brothel. Some writers think that she was the one who by her risqué and scandalous conduct provided John with the imagery of harlotry.

John sees that the woman is drunk. It is not wine, however, that has caused her condition. She is **drunk with the blood of the saints,** those who have sacrificed their lives in faithful wit-ness to Jesus. John is astonished. The vulgarity of the scene is more than he can cope with. As an expression of the true nature of the Roman empire, the whore is overpoweringly repulsive.

7-8   In response to John's amazement the angel agrees to ex-plain the mystery of the woman and the beast. In reverse order, the beast is interpreted first (vv. 8-14) and then the woman (v. 18).

Of the beast it is said that he **once was, now is not, and will come up out of the Abyss.** This appears to be in deliberate contrast to the glorified Christ of chapter 1 who said, "I am the Living One; I was dead, and behold I am alive for ever and ever!" (1:18; see 2:8; also the description of God in 1:4, 8 and 4:8). Deception is a major ploy of Satan's henchmen (13:13-15). Since for John the beast was Rome, the persecutor of faithful believers, this description of the beast would indicate that while the church at an earlier time had experienced hostility, at the moment it found itself in a period of temporary relief (the beast **once was,** but **now is not**). However, the beast **yet will come** (v. 8).

In A.D. 60 Nero was that beast. He instigated a persecution of the Christians in order to avert suspicion that he had set fire to Rome. Both Peter and Paul were victims of this cruel hoax.

In John's day the church was on the verge of a renewed persecution under Domitian. The beast was about to rise from the Abyss.

Whenever in the course of history secular power oversteps its lawful bounds and tyrannizes the innocent, it can be said that the beast has risen from the Abyss. At the end of history he will rise one final time to launch an all-out assault against the people of God. On that occasion he will be confronted by the King of kings, who will destroy him from the face of the earth and dispose of him forever in the fires of perdition (cf. 19:20).

John reports that those whose names are not written in the book of life will be **astonished when they see the beast.** His recuperative powers are incredible. Evil seems to return from every defeat with renewed vigor, surviving every deathstroke (13:3) to wage war again.

9-11 From this point on, the angel's explanation of the beast becomes more difficult to follow. Anticipating what is to follow, the angel announces, **"This calls for a mind with wisdom."** A similar statement (13:18) accompanied the designation of 666 as the number of the beast. Neither section is crystal clear!

The angel explains that the seven heads of the beast are **seven hills on which the woman sits.** The first-century reader would immediately recognize a reference to Rome, the city built upon seven hills. So far, so good. But now the angel goes on to say that the seven heads are **also seven kings.** The symbolism of apocalyptic literature must never be approached as if it were some sort of inflexible linguistic code. Symbols are fluid and have a way of conforming to the contours of the immediate context. The seven heads are seven hills and seven kings simultaneously.

The plot thickens. Five kings have fallen, one currently is, and the seventh — when he comes — will remain only for a short time. What does all of this mean?

Many writers take the seven kings to be a series of Roman emperors, with John living during the reign of the sixth. If it is true that John writes during the reign of Domitian (A.D. 81-96), it is possible to make him number six only by beginning with Caligula (A.D. 37-41) rather than Augustus (30 B.C.–A.D. 14) and skipping the three who ruled in quick succession during the brief period between Nero (A.D. 54-68) and Vespasian (A.D. 69-79). This interpretation is as defective as the arithmetic brought in to support it. Equally unsatisfactory is the attempt to depict the seven kings as seven kingdoms.

The most reasonable approach is to see the seven kings as symbolizing the power of Rome as an historic whole. Seven is the number of completeness. To be living under the sixth king with the prospect that the seventh will rule for only a short time is a way of saying that the end of secular abuse and persecution is at hand. Roman domination is drawing to a close. God will soon intervene to vindicate the faithful and bring judgment upon the persecutors.

Verse 11 is the heart of the riddle. The beast is described as an **eighth king** who **belongs to the seven.** He is not simply one of the seven. While in one sense he belongs to the seven (he rules on earth as a king), in another sense he is distinct. As an eighth he stands outside and above the historical sequence of secular powers that have governed the empire up through John's day. In short, the beast is not a human ruler through whom the power of evil expresses itself — he is that evil power itself. The beast is none other than Antichrist, that malign and evil being who throughout the history of the church has set himself in opposition to the people of God (1 John 2:18). But he is **going to his destruction.** No matter how terrible the beast may appear and how intimidating his claims, this oppressor will receive his just reward in the eternal fires of retribution.

12-14 The **ten horns** of the scarlet beast are said to be **ten kings who have not yet received a kingdom.** When they do acquire power and authority (even though it will be for a brief period only — **one hour**), they will turn it over to the beast. These ten kings are symbolic of the totality of all secular power in the last days. They will join forces with the Antichrist to **make war against the Lamb.** This great confrontation will take place when Christ, the warrior Messiah, returns to establish his sovereignty over the rebellious world order (19:11-21).

The angel declares that the Lamb will overcome the vast coalition of earthly powers because he is **Lord of lords and King of kings.** No force on earth can withstand the greatness of his power. He rules over all. With him will be his followers — the **called,** the **chosen,** and the **faithful.** As they have been true to him in times of severest testing, they will share with him in his ultimate triumph over wickedness. The beast is to go down in defeat before the Lamb. Those who by faith have weathered the storm of Satanic opposition will stand with their leader in his moment of victory.

15-18 The interpreting angel ends his extended discourse on the beast and identifies the harlot and the waters upon which she sits. The **waters** are **peoples, multitudes, nations and languages** — in other words, the entire inhabited world. No nation has successfully resisted the seduction of the harlot Rome. All have become entangled in devious alliances with the world's most powerful prostitute.

But now a sudden political shift takes place. Whereas the ten kings had given their authority to the scarlet beast and joined in battle against the Lamb, they now turn in fierce hatred against the prostitute. The rebellion of the kings reflects the law of political history that every revolution carries within itself the seeds of its own destruction. The fierceness of their hatred for the one who has brought them to defeat is seen in their vicious acts of retaliation. They strip her **naked, eat her flesh,** and **burn her** remains with fire — a ghastly ordeal that reveals man's evil nature striking out in blind fury against the supposed cause of its own wickedness.

The angel adds that God has put it into the hearts of the kings to carry out his purpose. In the final analysis, even the destructive wrath of the wicked is used by God to fulfill his word.

Almost as an afterthought, the angel says that the **woman in the vision is the great city that rules over the kings of the earth.** Rome is that wicked harlot who has seduced the political powers to meet their own destruction.

Revelation 18

Chapter 18 is a prophetic portrayal of the destruction of Rome. Since the various speakers in the chapter draw heavily from the prophetic oracles and taunt songs of the Old Testament, the NIV prints about two-thirds of the chapter in poetic form. The fall of Rome is described in the lyric prose of prophets who raised their voices against the enemies of God's covenant people, Israel.

Some writers feel that the tone of the chapter is too vindictive to be genuinely Christian. Such criticism fails to take into account the nature of prophetic realism. Chapter 18 is portraying the ultimate collapse of an evil and cruel anti-Christian world order. Its rhetoric is appropriate to its message and must not be interpreted apart from its prophetic background.

1-3 John sees an angel descending from heaven. The angel possesses an authority equal to the awesome task of announcing the complete overthrow of all secular power. Coming from the presence of God, the angel illuminates the earth with divine splendor. We are reminded of Moses, who found it necessary to veil himself when he returned from God's presence. The radiance that shone from his face frightened the Israelites who had been disobedient during his time on Mount Sinai (Exod. 34:29-35).

The angel calls out with a mighty voice, **"Fallen! Fallen is**

Babylon the Great!" The words echo Isaiah 21:9. This declaration is true whenever the forces of evil are put to rout. In the last days "Babylon" will fall in a final and ultimate sense. The angel proclaims this event as already having taken place because from a prophetic standpoint what God decrees will of necessity transpire. It lies beyond any possibility of change.

Since Babylon has fallen, the victory has already been won. The forces of Antichrist may go through the motions of conflict, but the outcome has been determined. God is sovereign, and history is under his control. The triumph of God over all the forces of evil is the major theme of the book of Revelation.

By portraying Babylon as a **haunt for every evil spirit** and **every unclean and detestable bird,** the author is saying that the once powerful and indulgent capital of world civilization is doomed to absolute desolation. Babylon has fallen because she has seduced the nations of the world to follow her corrupt and immoral life-style.

4-8 Another voice from heaven is heard. The people of God are called to come out of the wicked city. Oracles against ancient Babylon by Isaiah and Jeremiah provide much of the rhetoric (consult a cross-reference Bible for specific parallels). Believers are to separate themselves from the great city that symbolizes arrogant power and wanton luxury. Why? So that they will not be seduced into sharing her wicked way of life and consequently receive her plagues. Historically the church has often been tempted to compromise its stand and come to terms with evil. Theology, in an attempt to be relevant, has frequently adjusted itself to the whims of culture and even gone so far as to support practices clearly contrary to revelation. God's way is not to conform to culture but to avoid every unholy alliance.

Babylon, the ancient Mesopotamian city on the Euphrates, symbolizes not only first-century Rome but the eschatological stronghold of secular power as well. Babylon stands for man in his defiant opposition to the ways of God.

Throughout history, the city appears wherever brute force and intrigue have been used to subjugate the many for the benefit of the few. The sins of Babylon have been **piled up** until they reach heaven itself. God remembers her many crimes, and Babylon is to be paid back in the currency of her wickedness. She is to receive **double for what she has done.** She offered her cup of immorality to the nations (14:8). Now she must drink the wrath of God from the same cup. She gave herself **glory and luxury**; now she is to receive a like amount of **torture and grief.**

Babylon is a proud and arrogant city. She boasts that she sits as a **queen,** not a **widow.** She is beyond personal loss. Her men do not lie dead on the field of battle. She will never have to mourn. "Not so," declares a voice from heaven. Plagues will suddenly overtake her. Without warning, death, mourning, and famine will be her lot. She is to be **consumed by fire** when the Lord God, the mighty One, comes in judgment. Nothing was quite so devastating in ancient times as a city on fire. Babylon is to be consumed by raging flames. In the coming judgment, all human opposition to God will be destroyed.

9-10 The next eleven verses are comprised of three separate dirges. The first lament is chanted by the kings of the world who have shared the luxury of Rome (vv. 9-10), the second by the merchants who have grown rich supplying her demands (vv. 11-17a), and the third by the maritime industry, which has delivered from abroad whatever she craved (vv. 17b-19). Note the strong resemblance to Ezekiel's lamentation over Tyre (Ezek. 27).

The **kings of the earth** who shared in Rome's illicit practices stand amazed as they watch the city burn. Not about to rush to the rescue of their mistress, they watch her torment **from far off.** Terrified, they bewail the sudden destruction of the once powerful capital of the world. The use of fire to depict the eschatological collapse of the world order is common in New Testament thought (see 2 Pet. 3:12). Throughout Scripture, fire is a symbol of judgment.

11-17a   The lament is next taken up by the **merchants of the earth.** Their sorrow is not for Rome but for the collapse of their own financial empires. With Rome in flames, who will buy their expensive merchandise? The impressive list of imports (vv. 12-13) emphasizes the excessive luxury of the capital city. Ancient sources report that many of the Roman emperors had an insatiable appetite for self-gratification. Nero spent $100,000 for Egyptian roses for a single banquet. It is reported that Vitellius spent $20 million (mostly on food) during his reign of less than one year. Small wonder that greedy merchants around the world bewail the destruction of their best market!

Like the kings of the earth, the merchants stand **far off,** terrified by the great city's torment and mourning her demise. Each group interprets the disaster in terms of its own special interests.

17b-19   The third group to lament the destruction of Rome consists of those connected with the maritime industry. When they see the smoke of her burning, they **throw dust on their heads** and mourn. Since Rome was the center of the shipping industry, all who made their fortunes from the sea established home port there.

20   Verse 20 is a momentary break in the narrative of Rome's fall. The **saints and apostles and prophets,** who are called upon to rejoice over her fall, do not represent the church on earth but the church glorified. In the opening phrase, it is **heaven** that is to rejoice. God has judged Rome for the way she has treated the church. In time every injustice will be punished. God would not be moral if he failed to requite the wicked for their selfishness and cruelty.

21-24   In verses 11 through 19, we saw the effect of Rome's fall on outsiders who were profiting from her excessive luxury.

In the following verses we see the effect of her fall on those who lived and worked within the city.

But first an act of prophetic symbolism: a mighty angel picks up a **boulder the size of a large millstone** and hurls it into the sea, saying that the great city of Babylon will be thrown down with equal violence. Babylon of course is Rome. And Rome in turn is the eschatological city of secular opposition to God. Both will suddenly disappear like a millstone thrown into the sea. God's reprisal against his enemies is sudden and devastating.

The completeness of Rome's destruction is seen in the recurring phrases **"will never be heard/be found/shine in you again"** (six times in vv. 21-23). Silence falls upon the city. The glad sounds of harp and trumpet, voice and flute, are never to be heard again. The sound of craftsmen plying their trade has stopped. The lights are off. Marriages have ceased. Judgment has fallen because Rome's deceitful merchants have led all the nations of the world astray. Rome is condemned because of her corrupt leadership and her immoral practices.

A final reason for Rome's fall is her persecution of the church. Her streets are red with the blood of Christian martyrs. As the center of opposition to Christ and the church, she is guilty of all innocent blood.

Revelation 19

For some time now, John's visions have been dark and foreboding. Chapter 16 pictured the seven bowls of God's wrath. Chapter 17 described the punishment of the great prostitute. Chapter 18 dealt with the destruction of Rome. Against this bleak background, we now hear what has appropriately been called the "Hallelujah Chorus" of chapter 19 (vv. 1-8).

The word "hallelujah" means "Praise the Lord." It is found only here in the entire New Testament. In chapter 18 we heard three laments (by kings, merchants, and seamen). Now, as though to balance the sorrowful dirges of those affected by the fall of Rome, three corresponding groups (a heavenly multitude, twenty-four elders and four living creatures, and a voice from the throne) raise their voices in praise and adoration of God.

1-5 The **great multitude** gives praise to God because he has condemned the harlot and avenged the blood of his servants. **Salvation and glory and power** belong to God because his judgments are **true and just.**

Rome has corrupted the nations of the world, enticing them into taking part with her in her illicit activities. She is also guilty of persecuting the Christian church. In the early days of Domitian, believers were living under the shadow of an approaching persecution. It would be comforting to know that before long God would retaliate against the state for its oppressive activities. No earthly power, not even the emperor himself, can put God's people to death and get away with it. God's judgment will be complete and final — **the smoke** [of the city] **goes up for ever and ever.**

The twenty-four elders and the four living creatures fall down and worship God (as they did when the Lamb received the scroll; cf. 5:6-10). They cry out, **"Amen"** (So let it be!), **"Hallelujah!"** (Praise the Lord!). The overthrow of evil and the vindication of righteousness receive the high praise of heaven. A voice from the throne calls for the servants of God — all who fear him, both small and great — to join in an anthem of praise. The conflict of the ages is over, and God has prevailed.

6-10 John's visions continue. Once again he hears what sounds like the voice of a great multitude. It must have made an unusual impression on him in that he goes on to describe it as the **roar of rushing waters** (a mighty cataract) and as **loud peals of thunder.** To grasp the overpowering and dramatic effect of this scene, we must imagine ourselves standing at the base of an enormous waterfall or in the midst of a violent thunderstorm.

The heavenly multitude (cf. 19:6 with 19:1) praises God because he has taken up his reign and **the wedding of the Lamb** has come. With the final defeat of sin, the reign of God has at last been fully established. While God is eternally sovereign, his actual control over men and nations is established and recognized as history moves toward its close — first by the work of Christ on the cross and then at the close of the age by the destruction of sin and Satan.

The concept of a marriage between God and his people has its roots in the Old Testament. Hosea 2:19, for example, records God's promise to Israel: "I will betroth you to me forever." In the New Testament, Paul describes the relationship between Christ and the church with the metaphor of marriage (Eph. 5:32). Now in Revelation, the multitude declares that the wedding of the Lamb has come.

In biblical times marriage involved two events separated by a period of several months. First came the betrothal (legal and binding), and then the wedding itself. The church is now betrothed to Christ. At his return the wedding will take place.

The bride is adorned in **fine linen, bright and clean.** She stands in marked contrast to the harlot of chapter 17, who was gaudily dressed in bright colors and expensive accessories (17:4). A parenthetical note explains that **fine linen stands for the righteous acts of the saints.** The adornment of the church consists in her obedient response to the many opportunities for compassion and loving service. This is not a doctrine of salvation by works. It is rather the thoroughly biblical principle that the true people of God must of necessity live transformed lives. They act righteously because they are in fact righteous (in Christ). A testimony of faith unsupported by a changed life is fraudulent.

The fourth beatitude in Revelation appears at verse 9. **"Blessed are those who are invited to the wedding supper of the Lamb."** That believers are portrayed as the bride of Christ as well as the wedding guests is typical of apocalyptic language. The style in which Revelation is written enjoys all the freedom of poetic expression. It appeals to the fluidity of imagination, not to the inflexibility of logic. The wedding supper is not a specific feast that takes place before the millennium. It depicts, rather, the eternal relationship between Christ and those who have accepted his love. The wedding supper lasts forever!

John falls prostrate at the feet of the angel. He would pay appropriate homage to this one who has declared the blessedness of all who have been invited to the wedding feast. But John is stopped short by the angel, who reminds him that he is simply a **fellow servant** with the apostle and with all those who hold to the witness that Jesus bore. God alone is to be worshiped. To this the angel adds that the message attested by Jesus is the essence of prophetic declaration. God is worshiped because he is the one who gives revelation; the angel is only a mediator and interpreter of visions.

11-16 At last we arrive at the central vision of the entire book of Revelation. The appearance of the Warrior-Messiah marks the end of the old order and the beginning of the new. It is the event for which the believing church has patiently waited over the course of some twenty centuries. The heavens are opened, and the conquering Messiah and his armies return to make war with the enemy.

A **white horse** appears. Its rider is called **Faithful and True.** The name reflects the fact that the fate of the beast and his followers is compatible with truth and justice. Retribution enacted by the Messiah is neither unfair nor out of line. He judges and makes war with perfect justice.

John's attention is immediately caught by the eyes of the rider; they are **like blazing fire.** Nothing remains hidden before his piercing gaze. On his head are **many** royal **crowns.** His sovereignty is unlimited. He bears a name that no one else knows. Writers have offered a number of suggestions about the name, only to prove what the text itself says: **no one but he himself** (that is, Christ) **knows** or understands the name. The name is intricately connected with the mystery of his being.

The Messiah is dressed in a **robe dipped in blood.** Although it is tempting to interpret this as the blood of Christ shed for the sins of man, in this context the blood is that of the Messiah's enemies. The imagery recalls a passage in Isaiah where God, in answer to the question "Why are your garments red?" answers that he has trampled Edom and Bozrah in his anger, and "their blood spattered my garments" (Isa. 63:1-6). Apocalyptic imagery is not squeamish.

The rider of the white horse is named **the Word of God.** The Hebrews did not think of a word as a mere sound but as an active agent that brought about what it declared. In Hebrews 4:12 the word of God is said to be "living and active . . . sharper than any double-edged sword." The Warrior-Messiah is God's final word to man. When God speaks, his will is actively carried out in time and space.

The **armies of heaven,** riding white horses and dressed in fine linen, follow their leader. They apparently take no active part in the ensuing warfare. The nations are struck down by a **sharp sword** that proceeds from the mouth of the Messiah. This sword stands for the word of judgment that Christ speaks (compare 1:16; 2:12, 16). We should not expect to see a literal sword protruding from the mouth of Christ at his Second Coming. We are dealing with apocalyptic images. The expression means that the Messiah's word of judgment slays like a mighty sword.

The Messiah will also rule the nations with a **iron scepter.** As the shepherd carried a stout rod to fend off the attacks of wild beasts, so Christ will destroy all the evil forces that have endangered the church through the ages. To "rule with a rod of iron" (AV) refers to the fact that he will destroy the nations, not govern them.

Christ will also tread the winepress of the fierce **wrath of God.** Retaliation is pictured in terms of a great flow of blood. In this context God is portrayed, not as a sentimental father who overlooks evil, but as a warrior who passionately hates all sin and injustice. The wrath of God is a thoroughly biblical doctrine and must never be watered down out of a desire to make him more palatable to modern man.

On his robe and on his thigh is the most exalted name imaginable: **KING OF KINGS AND LORD OF LORDS.** Handel has captured the grandeur of this title in his magnificent "Hallelujah Chorus." Whatever kings may be, God is yet their king. Whatever lords may exist, God is still their lord. He rules supreme over all earthly powers. He is Lord and Master of all creation.

17-21 In one way or another, each of the visions in Revelation has brought us closer to the end. Now, just before the final battle, one last vision heightens even further our anticipation of the culmination of human history. An angel is seen standing in the sun. He delivers a grisly invitation to the birds of prey

101

circling in mid-heaven awaiting the carnage: "Come to **the great supper of God** and gorge yourself on the flesh of man and beast." No one is to be spared. Both free and slave will fall in battle. Even kings and generals will go down. The earth will be covered with the bodies of men and their horses. The prospect of being left on the field of battle at the mercy of predators was abhorrent to warriors of old. This grim "supper of God" provides a dramatic contrast to the joyful "wedding supper of the Lamb" (v. 9).

Armageddon has arrived. The beast and his armies are matched against the Messiah and his followers. The moment of truth is here. But strangely, no conflict is described. Instead, we simply learn that the beast and the false prophet are captured and **thrown alive into the fiery lake of burning sulfur.** There has never been any real question about the outcome of this final confrontation. Satan was defeated on the cross, and those who have prolonged his cause will share in his defeat.

We will remember that the beast is the personification of secular power in its opposition to righteousness, and the false prophet is pseudoreligion as it persuades men to accept and worship this power. Both are consigned to the lake of fire. Punishment by fire is a common theme in Jewish apocalyptic writing. A lake of fire is mentioned in the Bible only in Revelation. It is undoubtedly the equivalent of hell, Gehenna, a place of fire inhabited by the wicked dead (cf. Mark 9:43-48).

The account closes by noting that the rest were killed by the sword that came out of the Messiah's mouth. The birds descend and gorge themselves on the flesh of the fallen. The gory ordeal is over, and the curtain descends on the stage of history.

Revelation 20

We come now to one of the most thoroughly discussed passages in the book of Revelation. Verses 1 through 6 of chapter 20 teach the doctrine of a millennium (or thousand-year period), during which time Satan will be locked up underground in the Abyss and Christ, with his followers, will reign on earth. Interpretations vary primarily on the basis of whether this reign is viewed as taking place at the present time (amillennialism) or whether it will follow the return of Christ (premillennialism). Strong arguments can be marshaled in support of either position.

This commentary follows the premillennial approach for several reasons. It is more in keeping with the apocalyptic outlook that underlies the imagery and thought patterns of the book. In addition, the events of chapter 20 follow quite understandably the victorious return of the Warrior-Messiah in chapter 19. There is no particular reason why this sequence of events should be interrupted. The history of interpretation reveals that amillennialism arose not so much as an attempt to explain the text but as an allegorical reaction to the extreme literalism of certain fringe groups in the third- and fourth-century church.

1-3 An angel descends from heaven with the key to the **Abyss** (an underground cavern that housed evil spirits awaiting judgment; see Jude 6). In his hand is a great chain. The angel seizes the devil, binds him, throws him into the Abyss, and then locks and seals the entrance. There Satan is securely imprisoned for the next one thousand years. The purpose of this restriction is that he might not deceive the nations any longer. Following this period of retention, he is to be set free for a short time.

Satan is described by four different titles. Not only is he **Satan** (the adversary), but he is also **the devil** (the accuser), **the dragon** (who, defeated in heavenly combat, vents his wrath against the church; 12:7-17), and **that ancient serpent** (who deceived Eve in the garden of Eden; Gen. 3). His names expose his true nature.

4-6   John now sees thrones upon which are seated those who have received the authority to judge. The text does not indicate who they are, or make clear exactly whom or what they are to judge. Those seated upon the thrones may comprise a heavenly court that is in some way connected with the great white throne judgment of verses 11 through 15.

John also sees the souls of those who had been executed for their faithful witness to Jesus and the word of God. They are further portrayed as not having worshiped the beast or his image. Neither have they received his mark on their foreheads or their hands. The description leads us to conclude that this group of martyrs is to be identified with the souls under the altar who, in 6:9-11 (the fifth seal), were calling upon God to avenge their blood. They represent every faithful witness whose testimony has resulted in death. It is with this group of martyrs that the millennium deals.

The martyrs are said to come to life and reign with Christ for a thousand years. It is crucial to determine what **came to life** means in this context. Those who interpret the millennium in a nonliteral sense (amillennialists) hold that it means to be resurrected from a state of spiritual death. Verses such as Colossians 3:1 ("Since, then, you have been raised with Christ") are used in support of their interpretation. From this it would follow that to "reign with Christ" would mean to share with him in this present age his sovereign control over the earth.

104

It is more natural, however, to take the crucial expression ("came to life") to mean a return to life in a physical sense. In Revelation 2:8 Christ is described as the one who "died and came to life again" (the same Greek verb). Jairus's daughter had died, but he knew that if Jesus touched her she would "live" (Matt. 9:18, the same Greek verb).

The most powerful argument that verse 4 speaks of a physical resurrection is that in the very next verse (v. 5) the same verb is used to describe the bodily resurrection that follows the millennium. There is no indication in the text that this crucial verb should be interpreted in two widely different ways in these adjacent passages.

Readers often ask if the thousand years should be taken as a literal period of time. On the one hand it is true that unless the plain sense makes nonsense, we should seek no further sense. Following this lead we would probably take the thousand years as one thousand actual years of 365 days each.

On the other hand, most of the numbers we have encountered thus far in Revelation have been symbolic. Seven designates completeness. The number 144,000 is a multiple of twelve, which is the number both of the tribes of Israel and of the disciples of Christ. In either case, one thousand years would be an extended period of time, during which Christ and the martyred saints would carry out their reign.

But what is the purpose of the millennium? The usual premillenarian answer is that it serves to demonstrate within history the victory of righteousness over evil. However, if it is true that the millennium has to do with Christian martyrs rather than the church at large, another explanation is to be preferred.

In chapter 6, the martyrs were told to wait under the altar until their number would be complete. Then their blood would be avenged upon the hostile world (6:9-11). If Revelation 20 deals specifically with this group, then the millennium will be a special reward to those who have been put to death because of their opposition to the demands of the Antichrist. During their lifetime they were victimized by the power of the state. When Christ returns, the situation will be reversed and they will be the ones who will rule over their oppressors.

Is it necessary for an actual one thousand-year millennium to take place in history, or may we understand it in terms of what it symbolizes? Since every promise must be expressed in the language and culture of its own time, it may be that the millennium, like the "streets of gold," will be realized in a less than literal sense. Whether literal or symbolic, it represents the ultimate vindication of those who have given their lives in faithfulness to Christ rather than honoring the demands of Antichrist.

By placing the first sentence of verse 5 in parenthesis, the NIV has correctly identified the **first resurrection** as that of the martyrs. If it is true that the millennium is the vindication of actual martyrs (rather than the entire church), then **the rest of the dead,** who are raised after the thousand years, would include both believer and unbeliever. In either case, a blessing is pronounced on those who have a part in the first resurrection. The **second death** (identified in v. 14 as "the lake of fire") has no power over them. Their lot is to serve as priests of God and to rule with Christ for a thousand years.

7-10 At the close of the millennial period, Satan is released from his prison. True to his nature, he goes out to **deceive the nations** into following him into battle against the people of God. The most reasonable explanation of this unexpected turn of events is that God wishes to demonstrate one more time that Satan's evil purpose will never change and that human nature is not altered with the passing of even a thousand years of divine rule.

Gog and Magog are singled out as examples of nations that join with Satan in the final revolt. In Ezekiel 38 and 39, Gog is not a nation but a prince who leads an invasion against

Israel. And from Genesis 10:2 we learn that Magog is one of the sons of Japheth. This shift from personal names to nations causes no particular problem for the one who is aware of the nature of apocalyptic literature. In Revelation, Gog and Magog are symbolic of all nations that join in the final assault upon God and his people.

So successful is Satan in his deceit that the number of those who follow him are like the sand of the seashore. They march across the breadth of the earth and surround the camp of God's people. Once again (cf. 19:11ff.), no battle is described. Fire comes down from heaven and devours the entire army. The devil, however, is not consumed by the fire. He is thrown into a lake of burning sulfur to share the fate of the beast and the false prophet (19:20). This unholy trinity is **tormented day and night for ever and ever.** Revelation provides no support for the idea of a limited period of punishment to be followed by annihilation. As unpalatable as it seems to some, the Bible teaches the eternal suffering of the damned.

11-14   The time for final judgment has come. John sees a **great white throne.** The one seated upon the throne is God the Father, although, on the basis of such verses as John 5:22, some have understood this figure to be Christ. Earth and sky flee from his presence. Depending upon the degree of literalness adopted by the interpreter, this cosmic upheaval is either (1) a poetic way of expressing creation's reaction to the majesty of God, or (2) a description of the physical dissolution of the universe (perhaps in preparation for the new heaven and earth that are about to appear; 21:1).

All the dead stand before the throne awaiting judgment. The books are opened. The dead are **judged according to what they have done as recorded in the books.** Final judgment is not arbitrary. It is based squarely upon the record of a person's life. Note that John is not teaching a doctrine of salvation by works. Salvation is based upon the grace of God and is received through faith in the redemptive work of Christ. The reality of that faith, however, is determined by the quality of life it produces (see also Rom. 2:6; 1 Pet. 1:17). We are saved by grace but we are judged on the basis of our works.

In addition to the books that record the deeds of men, another book was opened — **the book of life** (v. 12b). While the relationship between these books is not absolutely clear, there is no doubt that the book of life is also involved in the judgment process. Verse 15 specifically says that those whose names are not found in the book of life will be cast into the lake of fire.

No one escapes judgment. The sea gives up its dead, as do death and Hades (the abode of the wicked dead). Once again we read that each person was judged **according to what he had done** (v. 13; cf. v. 12). Then all the wicked are thrown into the lake of fire along with death and Hades. Sin is put away forever, and everything associated with it is assigned to eternal punishment — Satan, who first rebelled against God (20:10); the beast and false prophet, who carried out his evil designs in history (20:10); the men of the world, who chose to worship Satan (20:15); death, his last weapon (20:14); and Hades, Satan's appropriate domain (20:14). The victory of God is complete!

Revelation 21

The final chapters of Revelation are radically different from the scenes of judgment we have just witnessed. Where sin no longer reigns, everything is totally transformed. The final two chapters of Revelation radiate the joy of the coming age. They portray the new heaven and the new earth, with only an occasional backward glance at those who have chosen to dwell outside the city of God (21:8; 22:11, 15). God's promise to "create new heavens and a new earth" (Isa. 65:17) is fulfilled in the descent of the heavenly Jerusalem as it takes its place on a renewed earth.

1-4 The renovation of the old order is a well-known theme in apocalyptic literature. Peter spoke of the coming day when the heavens will be destroyed by fire, and the elements will "disintegrate in fearful heat" (2 Pet. 3:12, Phillips). They will be replaced by a new heaven and a new earth in which "uprightness will have its permanent home" (2 Pet. 3:13, Williams). John now sees the final outcome of this cosmic transformation. The **sea,** which in Revelation is associated with all kinds of evil (note that the beast came out of the sea, 13:1, 6-7), will have no place in the new order.

John watches as the New Jerusalem (**the Holy City**) descends from heaven. It is adorned as a bride for her husband. The **new Jerusalem** symbolizes the people of God in their perfected and eternal state. It emphasizes that the church universal is a community of redeemed individuals living together in love.

A loud voice from the throne declares, **"Now the dwelling of God is with men."** The Greek word *skēnē* ("tabernacle") is closely related to the Hebrew word *shekinah* (the presence and glory of God). God himself in all his glory has come to take up his eternal residence with faithful believers. As the text says, **he will live** (*skēnōsei*, "tabernacle") **with them . . . and be their God.** This is the essence of heaven — not streets of gold or elaborate mansions of glory. Unbroken fellowship is the central feature of the eternal state.

God will wipe away **every tear.** These are not tears of remorse but the fading consequence of our passage through a sinful world. The old order with its death and mourning, crying and pain, has passed away. The new and perfect order of eternal joy has taken its place.

5-8 God declares from his throne that he is **making everything new.** The old order, marred by sin, fades into the past. God instructs John to write down his words, for they are trustworthy and true. Future blessedness has become present reality. **"It is done,"** he exclaims. Sin has been put away forever, and righteousness reigns supreme throughout the new heaven and earth.

God is **the Alpha and the Omega** (the first and last letters of the Greek alphabet). He is the source of all things and their ultimate goal. He is **the Beginning and the End.** To all who are thirsty, God gives **to drink without cost from the spring of the water of life.** He promises spiritual refreshment and eternal felicity to all the thirsty who come to him. He will accept the overcomer as his **son** and will be **his God.** All these metaphors add dimension and significance to our understanding of that which awaits the faithful in the world to come.

In stark contrast to the eternal family of God are those who, having chosen to join forces with the enemy, end up in the lake of fire. Many, perhaps all, of those listed in verse 8 are to be understood as professing Christians who gave up the faith. The **cowardly** had drawn back from following Christ when the going got rough. The **unbelieving** had denied their faith under pressure. The **vile** were polluted with the defilements of emperor worship. The **sexually immoral** had fallen into the major vice of paganism. These apostates (and the others mentioned in v. 8) have their place in the **fiery lake of burning sulfur.** This is the **second death**; it seals their doom forever. The purpose of the catalog of vices is to emphasize, by way of contrast, the righteous character of God's chosen people.

9-14 One of the angels who poured out the seven bowls of God's wrath now invites John to come and see **the bride, the wife of the Lamb.** The invitation parallels 17:1 in which the angel invited John to witness the punishment of the great whore. The bride and the harlot are set in vivid contrast. The New Jerusalem descends from heaven representing all that is sacred and beautiful. Rome symbolized the essential wickedness of human civilization here on earth.

In order to watch the descent of the Holy City, John is carried away in the Spirit to **a mountain great and high.** Mountains have always played an important role in God's dealings with man. Moses received the commandments on Mount Sinai (Exod. 20). Ezekiel's vision of a restored Israel came when he was on "a very high mountain" (Ezek. 40:2). Christ was taken to heaven from the Mount of Olives, and to that mountaintop he will again return (Acts 1:9-12).

The bride that John is to see turns out to be a city. Apocalyptic metaphors are mixed and show little inclination to conform to any literalistic system of interpretation. The faithful are portrayed not only as the bride of the Lamb but also as the eternal city in which God is to dwell.

The **Holy City** is aglow with the glory of God. It sparkles with the brilliance of precious jewels. A **great, high wall** symbolizes complete security. The city has **twelve gates,** inscribed with the names of the twelve tribes of Israel, and **twelve foundations,** upon which are written the names of the twelve apostles of the Lamb. It is obvious that by this imagery the author wishes to emphasize the continuity between Israel of old and the New Testament church. God's people from every age will share together in the glorious time to come. Twelve gates suggest abundant entrance, and twelve foundations, with the names of the twelve apostles, remind us that the church is built upon the witness of the apostles and prophets (see Matt. 16:18; Eph. 2:20).

15-17 The angel in charge of showing John the New Jerusalem has a rod of gold with which he measures the city, its gates and its wall. The city is laid out like a square, as long as it is wide. But it is also said to be **as wide and high as it is long.** This means that the city of John's vision is a cube. The shape would immediately remind the Jewish reader of the inner sanctuary of the temple, a perfect cube measuring some thirty feet in each direction. In this Most Holy Place dwelt the very presence of God. A city shaped like a cube would symbolize God's eternal dwelling with man.

The enormous size of the city has caused some surprise. Since a stadion is about 607 feet, **12,000 stadia** would be approximately 1,400 miles. While it is possible to imagine a city large enough to cover all of the United States west of the Mississippi, it is next to impossible to think of the same city as reaching 1,400 miles up into the ionosphere. Obviously, the numbers are symbolic. They portray the New Jerusalem as an enormous city; we are not expected to take the measurements in a literal fashion. The same can be said of the walls of the city, which are **144 cubits** (about 216 feet) high (NIV has "thick," but there is no word in the Greek indicating either height or breadth). Two hundred-foot walls around a city more than seven million feet high would be extremely disproportionate! The number 144 is the square of twelve (the number both of the tribes and the apostles) and apparently was chosen for that reason.

18-21 The wall of the city is made of jasper, while the city itself is of pure gold. The foundations of the wall are inlaid with every kind of precious stone. Although it is difficult to identify and catalog the gems of antiquity with any precision, the stones listed would probably reflect such colors as green, blue, red, white, yellow, and purple. The gates of the wall are each made of a single pearl. The street is **pure gold.** The overall impression is one of beauty and brilliance. The city is magnificent. It is the dwelling place of God.

22-27 A great truth is enshrined in the fact that there is no temple in the eternal city. No temple is needed because **the Lord God Almighty and the Lamb are its temple.** Symbol has given way to reality. The temporary forms of this world have no continuing purpose in eternity. God and the Lamb are the temple. No other is needed. Nor does the city need sun or moon. It is illuminated by the glory of God. The Lamb is its source of light.

Verses 24-26 present a small problem. Who are the **nations** that walk by its light and the **kings of the earth** who bring their splendor into it? Who are the **impure** who will never enter its gates? (The problem exists in 22:2, 15 as well.)

The answer is that John is speaking of the future, using terms that belong to his own period in time. The references are not intended to teach that in the age to come certain people from the outside will have limited access to heaven. Rather, the eternal city is described as if it belonged to this earthly sphere of existence.

To say that kings and nations bring their tribute to the heavenly Jerusalem is to underscore the prominence and prosperity of the city. Its gates will never be shut because evil will no longer exist. There will be perfect security. That which is impure, shameful, and deceitful will be forever removed from the city. Only those whose names are written in the **Lamb's book of life** will enter.

Revelation 22

That a new chapter begins at this point tends to obscure the fact that the description of the New Jerusalem, which began at the ninth verse of chapter 21, continues on through the fifth verse of chapter 22.

1-5 The guiding angel (see 21:9, 15) shows John a river, clear as crystal, that flows out from the heavenly throne and down the center of a wide boulevard. The river of the water of life comes from the **throne of God and of the Lamb.** Note that the throne belongs to both God and the Lamb. On either side of the river stands a **tree of life,** bearing twelve different kinds of fruit and yielding a fresh crop each month. God's provisions for man in the heavenly city are varied and abundant.

Not only does the tree of life provide fruit for enjoyment, but its leaves are for **the healing of the nations.** This detail does not imply that in the age to come all the nations of the world will be healed from the sickness of sin. As we noted before (21:24-27), this kind of reference projects into the eternal state imagery that belongs to the present. The point John wishes to make is that there will be no disease in heaven. Neither will there be any curse.

God and the Lamb will rule the eternal city. The faithful will serve God, and their greatest joy will be to **see his face.** In ancient times criminals were banished from the realm so that they could never again see the face of the king (cf. Esth. 7:8). To see God is a blessing reserved for the pure in heart (Matt. 5:8), and will be fully realized only when we are transformed into his likeness (1 John 3:2).

Night will be no more. There will be no need of either lamp or sun because the radiance of God will illuminate every portion of the heavenly city. It is in this place of beauty and splendor that the church of Jesus Christ is to reign forever and ever.

6-7 Verses 6 through 21 are an epilogue to the entire series of visions that make up the book of Revelation. You will notice a number of similarities between the epilogue and the prologue (for instance: the book is a genuine prophecy, cf. 1:3 with 22:6; it is to be read in the churches, cf. 1:11 with 22:18; and it is for the encouragement of the faithful, cf. 1:3 with 22:12).

The angel declares that the visions of things to come are **trustworthy and true.** They merit our confidence because they correspond to reality. The source of revelation is God, who quickens the spirits of the prophets. The angel was sent by God to show his servants the things that **must soon take place.** It has troubled some interpreters that, from John's position in history, these things apparently did not take place **soon.** Some two thousand years have gone by, and the end is not yet.

The most satisfactory answer to the problem is that since the beginning of the church era we have been in the last days (Heb. 1:2). Throughout history the end has always been imminent in the sense that at any point in time this age could rapidly come to a close. This fact has lent an air of urgency to the church's mission of evangelism. From God's perspective, time is not a sequence of passing moments but an accommodation to the limitations of creation. He himself "inhabits eternity" (Isa. 57:15). He was, he is, he shall be. It is also helpful to note that predictive prophecy regularly involves a telescoping of time. The great redemptive events of God in time are brought together in the perspective of the prophet. Thus the consummation toward which history inevitably moves is always imminent in prophetic declaration.

Jesus says, **"Behold, I am coming soon!"** (vv. 7, 12). In times of stress this truth has brought great encouragement to faithful believers. In times of rejoicing it has heightened the church's anticipation of the glorious age to come.

The two last beatitudes in Revelation (there are seven altogether) are found in chapter 22. The first (v. 7) pronounces a blessing upon those who obey the prophetic message contained in the book. Prophecy is not given so that believers will be able to develop an elaborate chronology of the last days, but so that they will be obedient to its ethical implications. The primary goal is to change conduct, not to inform the intellect.

8-9 John, the author of Revelation, attests that he has heard and seen the things about which he has written. They are not literary creations conjured up to communicate religious insights. John is a recorder of actual visions; he is not a fanciful visionary. He falls at the feet of the angel who has been his guide, intending to worship him (curious, in view of 19:10!). But the angel prevents him. He too, along with John and all those who obey the words of the prophecy, is a servant of God. God alone is worthy of worship.

10-11 In an earlier era, the prophet Daniel was told to "close up and seal the words of the scroll until the time of the end" (Dan. 12:4). But now, that time has come, and John is instructed, **"Do not seal up the words of the prophecy of this book."** From the perspective of the seer, the end is so near that there is no longer opportunity for men to change their habits or alter their character. The destiny of each has been determined by the quality of life he has lived. The wrong will continue to do wrong.

Equally true is the fact that those who do right will continue to do right, and those who are holy will continue in holiness. The future has already been determined by the way each person has lived. There exists no possibility of a last-minute transformation.

12-13 Again we hear Christ declare that he is **coming soon.** He brings with him his **reward** and distributes it on the basis of what each person has done. In 20:12, judgment depended on the record of what men had done. Here we learn that rewards are given on the same basis. Perfect justice will be enacted because the One who distributes the rewards has complete knowledge: he is **the Alpha and the Omega . . . the Beginning and the End.**

14-15 The final beatitude of the book (v. 14) is pronounced on those who **wash** (the present tense suggests a continual washing) **their robes.** They are those who steadfastly refuse the temptation to soil their garments by compromising with sin and Satan. As a result, they have **the right to the tree of life.** Eternal life is their reward for faithfulness under trial. Or, put in another way, they may pass through the gates and on into the city of God.

Not so the wicked. Outside the city are all kinds of evil persons — dogs (the unclean), sorcerers, the sexually immoral, murderers, idolaters, and deceivers. No sinner of any sort will have a place within the eternal city. As we learned elsewhere (20:15), their end will be the lake of fire.

16 Jesus authenticates the angel who has guided John through the various visions of Revelation. The message has been for the churches. It is intended for their encouragement and direction in times of great stress. It assures the church universal that God is sovereign and will at the end of time destroy every vestige of wickedness and usher in the eternal age of righteousness.

By naming himself **"the Root and the Offspring of**

David," Jesus lays claim to the messianic promise given through the prophet Isaiah (Isa. 11:1, 10). He is also **"the bright Morning Star"** (see Num. 24:17) that heralds the end of the long night of tribulation and the dawn of a new day of eternal joy.

17   Verse 17 is a multiple invitation. **The Spirit** (the Holy Spirit) **and the bride** (the church) **say, "Come!"** Those who hear repeat the invitation. Whoever is thirsty may come. Whoever wishes may take as a free gift **the water of life.** Readers of the Old Testament will recognize a similar invitation extended by Isaiah, "Come, all you who are thirsty. . . . Come, buy wine and milk without money and without cost" (Isa. 55:1). The invitation in Revelation is general and extends to all who will hear the words of the prophecy.

18-19   John brings his apocalypse to a close with a severe warning against tampering with its contents. He warns that if anyone adds to the words of the prophecy, God will add to him the plagues described in the book. If anyone takes words away from the prophecy, God will take away from him his share in the tree of life and in the Holy City as described in the book.

The revelation of God's victory over evil, the return of Christ, the punishment of the wicked, and the eternal blessedness of the righteous — all will take place exactly as described. There is no possibility of the slightest change. For man to alter the prophecy by addition would be to involve God in saying something he never intended. To take away from the prophecy would be to deny God the right to say something he wants to say. Hence the seriousness of the warning. (It is a warning that should cause every commentator on Revelation to do his prayerful best in telling others what the book is all about!)

20   Revelation began with the promise that the consummation of history would "soon take place" (1:1). It closes with Christ's promise, **"Yes, I am coming soon."** John adds, **"Amen. Come,**

Lord Jesus." This prayer expresses the central hope of all faithful believers. It is the equivalent of the Aramaic *maranatha* ("Our Lord, come!") of 1 Corinthians 16:22, RSV.

21 Although Revelation is an apocalypse, it began as an epistle (1:4) and ends accordingly with a benediction. The benediction was first pronounced upon all those believers in the seven churches of Asia who listened while the book was read aloud. It now extends to all who love his appearing. From John's day until ours it has bestowed the grace of the Lord Jesus upon those who have steadfastly refused to be taken in by the propaganda of Satan or be intimidated by his threats. The people of God are those who have emerged victorious from the battle of faith. They are the overcomers who, in the face of persecution, have reaffirmed their commitment to the Lamb of God and his redemptive work in history.

Study Questions

The purpose of these Study Questions is twofold. If you are reading or studying this commentary by yourself, they should help you grapple with the meaning of Revelation and the relevance of its teachings for you today. On the other hand, if you are a member of a class or study group, they should give you ample material for reflection and discussion, both of the biblical passage itself and of this commentary. The leader may decide beforehand which questions to discuss during the meeting and how much time to devote to each.

Chapter 1

1. What does the word "revelation" mean and what is revealed in the final book of the New Testament?

2. What are the implications of the sovereignty of God in reference to the evil in the world?

3. How would you explain the choice of the seven specific cities to which the book of Revelation is addressed?

4. What were the historical circumstances that explain the title "faithful witness" as applied to Jesus? Are you able to envision a similar situation developing in the twentieth century?

5. On what basis can the death of Christ be called an exodus?

6. What is intended in the reference to God as "the Alpha and the Omega"?

7. Why was John exiled to Patmos?

8. Why do we call Sunday "the Lord's Day"? What does this imply about how we are to spend our Sundays?

9. Explain the two ways of interpreting verse 19. Which interpretation do you prefer, and why?

10. On what basis can congregations be referred to as "lampstands" and angels as "stars"? On the basis of these clues should Revelation be interpreted in a straightforward literal manner as "pre-written history"?

Chapter 2

1. What does it mean that Christ "walks among the seven golden lampstands" and "holds the seven stars in his right hand"?

2. On what basis was it appropriate for the church at Ephesus to test those who claimed to be apostles? Should the contemporary church test its leadership in much the same way?

3. Describe the first love that the Ephesian church had forsaken.

4. Does attention to correct doctrine necessarily rule out a close personal relationship with God? Suggest some practical ways by which the believer may overcome this problem.

5. How can memory help in regaining a previous level of spiritual life?

6. What does God do when believers refuse to repent of their lack of love? Explain.

7. What does it mean to be an overcomer?

8. In what way were the Christians at Smyrna rich?

9. What does it take to be a "real Jew"?

10. What do you think would take place if all Christians in America were called upon to renounce their faith or suffer the consequences? Do you think that this could happen within our lifetime?

11. On what basis can it be said that the "ten days" in verse 10 should be taken in a figurative sense?

12. What does it mean that Christ wields "a double-edged sword"?

13. What was the teaching of Balaam? Can you cite any contemporary examples of this error? Explain.

14. How does God deal with the church that tolerates doctrinal error and immoral conduct?

15. Explain "hidden manna" and "white stone."

16. Why did John refer to the heretical prophetess of Thyatira as Jezebel?

17. What is promised to the overcomer at Thyatira? If this were to be interpreted literally, when would it probably take place?

18. Which of the strengths (or weaknesses) mentioned in the first four letters are most characteristic of your local congregation?

19. Which of the first four churches would you rather join? Why?

Chapter 3

1. Describe the characteristics of the church that has the reputation of being alive but is in fact dead?

2. Does Christ come in judgment today on unrepentant churches? What kind of judgment does he mete out?

3. To what do white garments refer?

4. What does having one's name erased from the book of life mean?

5. Into what does the "open door" of verse 8 lead? Explain from the context.

6. What does John mean by his reference to "the synagogue of Satan"?

7. What is "the hour of trial" that is about to come on the

whole earth? In what way will believers be kept from this period of testing?

8. What is the meaning of each of the three names inscribed on the overcomers in verse 12?

9. What does it mean that the Laodicean church was lukewarm?

10. What is God's response to lukewarmness in the church at Laodicea? Is this still his response to lukewarmness in Christianity today?

11. How would you describe the Laodiceans' attitude toward their accomplishments? How can people be so self-deceived?

12. Explain how rebuke and discipline may be expressions of love.

13. To whom is Christ speaking in verse 20?

14. When will overcomers sit with Christ on his throne?

Chapter 4

1. Why is John summoned to heaven?

2. Why is it unlikely that John's heavenly summons represents the rapture of the church?

3. What does it mean to be "in the Spirit"?

4. What was the first thing John saw in heaven, and what does it symbolize?

5. Explain why the twenty-four elders should not be equated with the twelve patriarchs of the Old Testament and the twelve apostles of the New.

6. Who or what are the "seven lamps" in verse 5?

7. Do you think the description of the four living creatures is to be taken literally or figuratively? Why?

8. Some early writers equated the four living creatures with the four Gospels. What is your response to that interpretation?

9. How does the praise of the living creatures differ from that of the elders?

10. How does the song of the elders correct the dualism of the Gnostics?

11. Chapter 4 pictures the worship of God from within the context of an Oriental culture. Describe the equivalent worship in contemporary terms.

Chapter 5

1. How did the scrolls of antiquity differ from modern books?

2. Why did John weep when no one was found worthy to open the seven-sealed scroll?

3. Explain the titles "Lion of the tribe of Judah" and "the Root of David."

4. What is meant by interpreting these titles messianically?

5. Why should we interpret the Lamb of chapter 5 in terms of Jewish apocalyptic rather than Jewish sacrificial ritual?

6. What do the "seven horns" and the "seven eyes" symbolize?

7. How does the praise offered by the elders in chapter 5 differ from their praise in chapter 4?

8. Why was the Lamb worthy to open the scroll?

9. In what two ways did the death of the Lamb affect the future of the human race?

10. For what purpose is the church "a kingdom of priests"?

11. In apocalyptic language, how many are "ten thousand times ten thousand"?

12. What is the largest crowd of people you have ever seen? Imagine all of them singing praises to God. Does that help you to envision the scene of heavenly adoration in verses 4-14?

13. What indication is there in verse 13 that the Lamb is honored equally with God the Father?

14. If the church on earth spent more time envisioning

the glories of the heavenly state, would it be more or less effective here on earth?

Chapter 6

1. What does the white horse and its rider symbolize? What clause in verse 2 provides the clue for this interpretation?

2. What do the rider's bow and crown symbolize?

3. Why is it true to life that the red horse follows the white horse?

4. To what extent has history been shaped by the first two horsemen?

5. Explain historically why a black horse normally follows the two previous horses?

6. Why was the rider of the black horse forbidden to "damage the oil and the wine"? What does this suggest about the sovereignty of God even in times of war?

7. What is symbolized by the four horsemen of the Apocalypse as a group?

8. Who are those "under the altar," and why are they there?

9. Why do the martyrs ask God to avenge their death?

10. How would you answer the charge that the attitude of the martyrs was less than Christian?

11. How did ancient people interpret great cosmic disturbances?

12. On what basis are we permitted to interpret the great upheavals of verses 12-14 in a less than literal fashion?

13. Why will unbelievers in the last days call for the rocks and mountains to fall on them?

14. Why is the concept of a wrathful Lamb not paradoxical?

Chapter 7

1. Explain what John means by "the four corners of the earth."

2. Why are the servants of God sealed?

3. Who are the "144,000"? Is the number to be understood literally or symbolically?

4. Identify and explain the irregularities in the listing of the twelve tribes.

5. What group makes up the Israel of God in the New Testament? What does this imply about the relationship between the Old and New Testaments?

6. What is the purpose of the second vision (vv. 9-16) in chapter 7?

7. Who are those in white robes?

8. What is "the great tribulation"?

9. Does this second vision support the view that the church will be raptured prior to the great tribulation?

10. In verses 15-17 the blessings of heaven are described in terms that had special significance for those living in first-century Palestine. What terms might be used in the twentieth century to convey the same idea?

11. How do you explain tears in heaven?

Chapter 8

1. How do you account for the silence that followed the opening of the seventh seal?

2. What is the purpose of the trumpets in chapter 8?

3. Explain the chronological approach to the three numbered visions (seals, trumpets, and bowls).

4. Explain the recapitulation approach to the numbered visions. What is the major argument in favor of this interpretation?

5. How may it argued from verses 3-5 that the prayers of the martyrs move God to act in judgment?

6. In terms of judgment, how do the trumpets differ from the seals?

7. What is the significance of the recurring mention of "a third"?

8. Since God is responsible for John's visions, why did John draw from the Old Testament and apocalyptic sources for many of his images?

9. Why is verse 12 not describing an eclipse?

10. How do the first four trumpet plagues differ from those that follow?

11. Will the church ever experience the direct outpouring of God's wrath? Why or why not?

Chapter 9

1. Why do we understand the "star" of verse 1 to be a person? What does this tell us about the proper way to interpret apocalyptic literature?

2. What is "the Abyss"?

3. Why will the demon locusts not affect the believers alive during the last days?

4. Why are those afflicted by the locust plague unable to die?

5. What qualities are suggested by the description of the locusts in verses 7-10?

6. What is the possible connection between the king of the Abyss and the practice of some of the Roman emperors?

7. Is there any significance to the fact that the request to unloose the angels of destruction comes from the golden altar? If so, what?

8. How does the mission of the cavalry differ from that of the locusts?

9. In your opinion, what determines whether the number "two hundred million" in verse 16 is to be taken in a literal or symbolic sense?

10. Why are verses 20-21 a sad commentary on human nature?

11. Why do people worship idols? What are some of the idols of contemporary culture?

Chapter 10

1. Why are there interludes between the sixth and seventh seal and the sixth and seventh trumpet?

2. Of what would the angel's legs "like fiery pillars" remind the Jewish reader?

3. What is one major difference between the little scroll of chapter 10 and the seven-sealed scroll of chapter 5?

4. What indicates that John may have kept notes during the period of his visionary experiences?

5. Why do you think that in every generation there have been those who felt that they were living in the final period before the end?

6. In biblical terminology, what is meant by a "mystery"? What is the mystery that will be accomplished in the day of the seventh trumpet?

7. Why would John be hesitant to approach the mighty angel?

8. Explain what is meant by the scroll being "sweet as honey" in the mouth but "sour" in the stomach.

9. What are the contents of the little scroll?

10. Would you be glad to learn that we are about to enter the final period of human history? In what ways would this be sweet? In what ways sour?

Chapter 11

1. Explain why "Remember the Alamo" has to do with bravery rather than a building. What does this say about the way we use words?

2. What is "the temple" in verse 1, and what does it mean to "measure" it?

3. Since the church will encounter severe opposition, in what sense can it be said to be protected?

4. Explain the source of the time period of forty-two months. What does it symbolize?

5. After which two Old Testament characters are the two witnesses modeled? How do we know this?

6. What do the two witnesses represent?

7. Who is "the beast"?

8. What is the significance of the fact that the beast "comes up from the Abyss"?

9. Why is not "the great city" of verse 8 simply first-century Rome? Why can it be called "Sodom and Egypt"?

10. What does it mean that the two witnesses are raised to life?

11. Why will the rapture of the church not be secret?

12. What will be the response of the unbelieving world to the rapture of the church?

13. What does it mean that "the kingdom of the world" becomes "the kingdom of our Lord and of his Christ"? How does this relate to the Lord's Prayer?

14. On what basis do the twenty-four elders praise God?

Chapter 12

1. What is the major purpose of chapter 12?

2. Who is the "radiant woman" of verse 1?

3. Who is the "red dragon"? What is the significance of the number seven as it is used in reference to his seven heads?

4. Who is the "male child," and what does it mean that he will rule with "a rod of iron"?

5. What event in the life of Christ is symbolized by the male child being snatched up to heaven?

6. In Revelation the desert represents a sanctuary for protection. What does a desert suggest to us today? What does this say about the need to interpret Revelation against its first-century background?

7. At what point in time does the "war in heaven" of verses 7-9 take place?

8. Why is it important for the believer to understand the essential antipathy between God and Satan?

9. What does the title "Satan" mean? In what way is Satan a "satan" today?

10. When Christians slander one another, would it be appropriate to call such behavior devilish? Why or why not?

11. What accounts for the devil's fury during the final period of history?

12. Why is God's protection of the church in the final days to be interpreted as spiritual rather than physical?

13. Who are "the rest" of the woman's offspring?

14. What explanation does chapter 12 provide for the suffering of believers in the final period of human history?

Chapter 13

1. What practice within the Roman empire may account for the blasphemous names inscribed on the seven heads of the beast?

2. The beast in John's vision was the Roman empire. What does it represent for us today?

3. Why do we believe that the beast has remarkable powers of recuperation?

4. Why do men worship the beast?

5. In what way will the beast blaspheme in the final period of history?

6. What does it mean to have one's name written in the Lamb's book of life?

7. What is taught by the proverbial statement in verse 10?

8. What does it mean that the second beast "comes out of the earth"?

9. Who are the three that constitute the evil trinity?

10. Explain the role of the false prophet.

11. What sets the stage for the great apostasy that precedes the return of Christ?

12. Explain *gematria.*

13. What do you think "666" stands for?

Chapter 14

1. Why does John introduce a vision of heavenly praise at this point?

2. What does it mean that the 144,000 have the name of the Lamb on their foreheads?

3. What is the theme of the new song sung by the 144,000? Why are the angels unable to sing this song?

4. What does it mean that the 144,000 "did not defile themselves with women"?

5. What is "the eternal gospel" proclaimed by the angel flying in midair?

6. Why should the inhabitants of the earth "fear God and give him glory"? On what basis can they be judged for not worshiping God?

7. Why does John refer to Rome as "Babylon"? Would it be fair to refer to modern America as "Babylon"? Why or why not?

8. Describe the nature of Rome's "adultery."

9. How can a God of love be said to be furious or wrathful?

10. What do verses 10-11 teach about hell.

11. Contrast the death of believers with the death of unbelievers.

12. On the basis of contemporary history, would you agree that secular power supported by the religion establishment leads to disregard for human rights? If so, cite an example.

13. Who is the reaper on the white cloud, and what does this final harvest depict?

14. Why in the Old Testament does the grape harvest offer an apt metaphor for divine wrath?

15. If the flow of blood in verse 20 is not to be taken literally, is it any less real? Explain.

Chapter 15

1. In what sense are the bowl plagues the last plagues?

2. Explain the statement that the seven bowls are the unfolding of the seventh trumpet.

3. How does one emerge victorious over the beast and his image?

4. What is the connection between "the song of Moses" and "the song of the Lamb"?

5. What does it mean that God is "King of the ages"?

6. Does the fact that all nations will come and worship God (v. 4) imply that in the end times the world will be converted to Christianity? Explain your answer.

7. Why is no one allowed in the temple until the bowls are poured out?

Chapter 16

1. Why have some scholars taken the trumpets and the bowls as covering the same sequence of events?

2. What event in Old Testament history supplies much of the imagery for the bowl plagues? How do you account for this?

3. Why are the people of God not mentioned during the bowl plagues?

4. Why is it appropriate for the followers of the beast to drink blood?

5. On what basis can it be said that the judgments of God are "true and just"?

6. One would think that scorching heat would cause unrighteous people to repent, but such is not the case. How do you explain such willful resistance?

7. Who are "the kings from the east"?

8. What tactics will be used by demonic spirits in the last days? Do you detect evidence of such activity in our day?

9. Who is speaking in the first part of verse 15? Does this verse imply that the church will be on earth until the final return of Christ? Explain.

10. What does "Armageddon" mean? "Har Magedon"?

11. What is the argument that this city (or mountain) is symbolic rather than geographic? Which interpretation do you favor? Why?

12. How would you explain the cataclysmic events connected with the seventh bowl plague?

13. What is man's response to the plague of hail? Does this surprise you or not? Why or why not?

Chapter 17

1. Explain what is meant by the statement that the harlotry of Rome was secular rather than religious?

2. Why did John consider the names covering the great prostitute to be blasphemous?

3. Why could Rome correctly be referred to as "Babylon"?

4. What made the prostitute drunk?

5. Explain the contrast between the beast and the glorified Christ of chapter 1.

6. Who was the beast in A.D. 60? Who is the beast today?

7. What does it mean that the beast "comes up out of the Abyss"?

8. What is so astonishing about the beast?

9. What two things are represented by the seven heads of the beast? Explain why this supports the position that the symbols of Revelation are not rigid but fluid?

10. List three different approaches to the problem of who or what is represented by the seven kings. Which seems most reasonable to you? Why?

11. In what sense does the beast belong to the seven kings yet is an eighth?

12. Who is the beast of the last days?

13. At what point in history will the ten kings join forces with the Antichrist?

14. What law of political history is illustrated by the rebellion of the kings and beast against the harlot?

Chapter 18

1. How would you argue against the person who says that the tone of chapter 18 is too vindictive to be Christian?

2. How can the angel declare that Babylon (Rome) has fallen since Rome was still standing when Revelation was written?

3. In what sense is the church called out of the corrupt world in which it lives? To what extent are believers expected to permeate society in order to win unbelievers to Christ?

4. What does it mean that Babylon symbolizes the eschatological stronghold of secular power?

5. What does Rome mean by claiming that she is "not a widow"?

6. At what point in time will all human opposition to God

be destroyed? Are you anxious for that day to come? Why or why not?

7. Why do the merchants and seamen mourn the fall of Rome?

8. What is portrayed by the mighty angel hurling a great stone into the sea?

9. List three reasons for the fall of Rome.

Chapter 19

1. Why does the great multitude declare, "Salvation and glory and power belong to our God"?

2. What does the word "hallelujah" mean?

3. Why does the "great multitude" (vv. 6-7) praise God?

4. Explain the Old Testament background for the "wedding of the Lamb." In what sense are the people of God married to him?

5. Contrast the adornment of the bride in chapter 19 with that of the harlot in chapter 17.

6. What is meant by the statement that the wedding feast depicts an eternal relationship and is not a specific feast prior to the millennium?

7. Why does the angel prevent John from worshiping him?

8. Who is the rider of the white horse? Is this the same white horse we met in chapter 6?

9. List the four names of Christ given in verses 11-16. What qualities do they represent?

10. Whose blood stained the robe of the Messiah?

11. How are we to interpret the "sharp sword" that protrudes from the mouth of the Messiah?

12. How do you explain the wrath of God in view of the fact that God is love?

13. Does the title "Lord of lords" imply the real existence of other lords? Why or why not?

14. Contrast "the great supper of God" (v. 17) with "the wedding supper of the Lamb" (v. 9).

15. Why is the battle of Armageddon not described at this point in chapter 19?

16. What is the fate of the beast and the false prophet?

Chapter 20

1. What is meant by the terms "amillennialism" and "premillennialism"? Which position do you favor, and why?

2. Does the imprisonment of Satan sound like a partial restriction of his activity or his complete removal from the arena of human affairs? Explain your answer.

3. What is meant by each of the four titles assigned to Satan?

4. Where in Revelation did we first meet a group of martyrs? From the description in verse 4, should we assume that the two groups are the same? Why or why not?

5. Do these martyrs come to life physically or spiritually? What is the basis for your answer to this question?

6. How long is the "thousand years" of Revelation 20?

7. According to most premillennialists, what is the purpose of the millennium?

8. If the millennium is taken symbolically, what would it represent?

9. If the millennium is the vindication of those who have lost their lives for the faith, who would be included in "the rest of the dead" (v. 5)?

10. Why is Satan released at the end of the millennial period?

11. Whom do "Gog and Magog" represent in the book of Revelation?

12. What expression in Revelation 20 argues eternal torment of the damned rather than annihilation?

13. On what basis are the dead judged? Doesn't this sound like salvation by works? Why not?

14. What purpose is served by "the book of life"?

15. What will be the final end of all evil? Why should this truth bring encouragement in times of trial?

Chapter 21

1. Explain what is meant by the cosmic transformation of the old order.

2. Who or what is the "new Jerusalem" that descends from heaven?

3. What is the essence of heaven?

4. Do you find joy and tears incompatible? Explain your answer.

5. What is claimed by the title "Alpha and Omega"?

6. Who are those described in verse 8?

7. What is meant by "the second death"? Why will there never be a third death?

8. Explain how "the bride, the wife of the Lamb" can turn out to be a city?

9. Describe the Holy City. In what way does this description emphasize the continuity between Israel and the New Testament church?

10. Why is it appropriate that the Holy City is in the shape of a cube?

11. Why should we understand the measurements of the city as symbolic?

12. What great truth is emphasized by the fact that there is no temple in the New Jerusalem?

13. How do you explain the existence of nations outside the city in the eternal state?

14. On what basis does a person gain entrance into the eternal city?

Chapter 22

1. What is symbolized by the tree that yields a different kind of fruit each month of the year?

2. Explain why there will be no disease in heaven.

3. What appears to be the greatest joy of heaven? To what extent are we able to enter into that experience now?

4. Explain in your own words why the promise of a soon return of Christ (v. 6) is not discredited by the historical fact that almost 2,000 years have passed since then.

5. Why is John told not to seal up the prophecy?

6. What provides a person the right to the tree of life?

7. What titles reveal that Jesus claimed to be the Messiah?

8. In what sense is Jesus "the bright Morning Star"?

9. What does it mean to "add to" or "take away from" the prophecy John has given? Can interpreters of the book of Revelation be guilty of either of these?

10. How do you account for the seriousness of the warning?

11. Why is it fitting that the book of Revelation closes with a benediction?

Subject Index

Subject Index

human nature 45-46, 81

idolatry 46
"in the Spirit" 3, 19
interlude 32, 47
interpretive clues viii, 5, 6, 25, 30-31

Jezebel 10-11
judgment 11, 57, 72-75, 79-82, 92-96, 107-8

key of David 15

lake of fire 102
Lamb: as conquering warrior, 100-102; as military leader, 24-25; worshiped, 70-71; worthy of adoration, 25-26; wrathful, 31
Laodicea, letter to 16-18
little scroll 48-51
Lion of the tribe of Judah 24
locusts, demonic 42-44
Lord's Day 3
lukewarmness 17, 18

male child 60
mark of the beast 68, 72
martyrs (martyrdom) 9, 29-30, 49, 53-54, 74, 87, 96, 104-6
Megiddo 83
Messianic promise 24
Messianic warrior 25
millennium 103-6
morning star 12, 118
Moses 54, 92
mystery of God 49-50

new age 12
new earth 109-19
new heaven 109-19
New Jerusalem 109-10, 112-13
Nicolaitans 7, 9
numbers, symbolic use of, 8, 26, 34; three and a half days, 55, 56; five

months, 43; forty-two months, 53-54, 63, 66; three and a half years, 53, 63; two witnesses, 53-56; twenty-four elders, 20, 57, 98; 144 cubits, 112; 666, 69; 1,260 days, 53-54, 60; 1,000 years, 105; 144,000, 32-34, 70-71; 200,000,000, 45

one hundred and forty-four thousand 32-34, 70-71
open door 15

pale horse 29
Patmos 3
Pergamum, letter to 9-10
persecution ix, 1, 8, 15, 35, 51, 59
Philadelphia, letter to 15-16
Polycarp 8
prayers of believers 39, 44
premillennialism 103
punishment, eternal 73, 107

rapture of the church 16, 19, 56
recapitulation 31, 37-39, 79
red dragon 59-63
red horse 28
reward 57
riddle 50-51
Rome 55 (*see* Babylon the Great; whore, the great)
Root of David 24

Sardis, letter to 13-14
Satan 60-62; binding of, 103; defeat of, 102; final revolt, 106-7; names of, 104
scroll of destiny 23-25
seal of God 42-43
seal sequence 27-31, 37, 48
sealing of the 144,000, 34
Second Coming 1, 3, 11, 14, 15, 100-101, 116, 117, 118
second death 9, 111

140